Leaves from a Family Tree

Leaves from a Family Tree

Joseph A. Ruskay

VANTAGE PRESS
New York

By the same author: *Halfway to Tax Reform*, Indiana University Press, 1970
(with Richard Osserman)

Published by Vantage Press, Inc.
516 West 34th Street, New York, New York 10001

Manufactured in the United States of America
ISBN: 0-533-11399-7

Library of Congress Catalog Card No.: 94-90887

0 9 8 7 6 5 4 3 2 1

Contents

Leaves from a Family Tree

FOREWORD AND ACKNOWLEDGEMENTS

I am deeply indebted to my late cousins, Dr. Burrill Crohn and Lawrence Crohn, whose writings I have extensively drawn on in this book. In Burrill's case the sources were *Notes on the Evolution of a Medical Specialist*, copyrighted in 1984 by his estate, *Burrill Bernard Crohn M.D., an Oral History*, printed by the American Gastroenterological Association in 1968, and a number of informal memoranda written from time to time by him about the Crohn family, including a June 1974 memoir with a foreword by his daughter, my cousin, Ruth Dickler. The late Lawrence Crohn was the principal author, assisted by his sister the late Marcella Rubel, of a chronicle *We Remember, a Saga of the Baum-Webster Family Tree*, written in January 1979, again with a preface by Ruth Dickler.

These have been invaluable sources of facts and data, especially about the huge Crohn family. I have also quoted most of a brief piece, again by Mrs. Dickler, about growing up with her famous father.

Further information was gleaned from *Horsecars and Cobblestones*, written by my mother Sophie Ruskay in 1948 and published by A.S. Barnes & Co., Inc. Another source was *The Songs of Paul Francis Webster*, published by the Hal Leonard Publishing Corporation and copyrighted by them in 1992. They granted me permission to quote the lyrics of the first chorus of "I've Got It Bad And That Ain't Good" by Paul Webster.

I spent the better part of two weeks examining the voluminous correspondence, speeches and other papers of the late Judith Epstein at the New York City archives of Hadassah, the Women's Zionist Organization, and wish to express my appreciation to Hadassah and to Ira Daly, the custodian of the archives, for making this material available to me. I am also indebted to the Center for Research on Women at Barnard College for guiding me to material in their library pertaining to women in the professions during the late 19th century and thereafter; and to Diane Ravitch, the author of *The Great School Wars*, which I found a valuable source of information about public school education in New York City during this same period.

I have reprinted with permission of *Reader's Digest* from its May 1970 issued (Copyright (c) 1970 by the Reader's Digest Association, Inc.), an item in "Personal Glimpses" about Dr. Burrill Crohn, contributed by Jean Kinney.

The New York Historical Society made available to me and permitted me to reproduce two photographs from their collection: one of Public School 157, and the opther of typical public school teachers at the turn of the century.

Numerous relatives and friends, including Fanny Cohen, Naomi Cohen, David Epstein, Professor Bettina L. Knapp, Guy Webster, Dr. Herbert Scheinberg, Janet Loeb and Toby Lelyveld have provided bits of information and suggestions for which I wish to thank them.

I wish especially to express my deep gratitude to Ruth Dickler, not only for making the writings of her father available to me, but for her professional advice when she read the various chapters as they were being written, and for her valuable suggestions and corrections.

Finally I am indebted to Ms. Scott Brown, a very talented and busy lady, for her skillful typing of the manuscript and its innumerable corrections and revisions.

CHAPTER I

THE RUSKAYS

Forbears

My father Cecil B. Ruskay liked to claim that his grandfather, Abbe Baum "laid his tefillin" (i.e. recited his morning prayers while binding his arm with the ritualistic leather phylacteries) "in the tent of Sitting Bull." While this was only one of Cecil's little jokes, the fact was that Abbe and his brother Israel had made their way to California in the middle of the last century and, on returning eventually to the East, traveled much of the way through hostile Indian territory.

The two Baum brothers had originally arrived in New York in 1842 as penniless Jewish immigrants fleeing Eastern Poland to avoid service in the army of the Czar. At that time all Europe was in the throes of a violent political upheaval culminating in the Revolution of 1848. All able-bodied young men were subject to military conscription, unthinkable for orthodox Jews required to obey dietary laws and to observe the Sabbath. Soon after arriving here they sent for their parents and sister, as well as their neighbor Jacob ("Yank") Webster and his family, and the two families found homes on East Broadway on New York's lower East Side. Abbe got a part-time job working for a small manufacturer of hand-painted ornaments. In addition, he worked as a scribe, writing out by hand in Hebrew, letter by letter and word for word on parchment scrolls, the text of the Bible, which became the Holy Torahs found in every synagogue.

Around 1850, with the news of the discovery of gold in California, the brothers decided to seek their fortunes in the West. According to a family chronicle written largely by a grandson, Lawrence Crohn, these two bearded pious Jews, armed with a small Torah for Sabbath and holiday prayers, and a supply of kosher food, embarked, along with scores of other adventurous souls, on a steamer for Panama. They crossed the isthmus by mule pack and made their way north by covered wagon caravan, with a military escort on the West Coast to guard against marauding Indians and unfriendly Mexicans. Arriving in Sacramento, they opened a small general store and traded clothing, shoes, knives, revolvers and other merchandise with the miners in exchange for gold dust. After a year or so they left California, wandered through Montana, and eventually worked their way back East in 1851 and rejoined their families.

Two years later the Baum and Webster families were united by marriage, Abbe marrying Goldie Webster, while his younger sister married "Yank" Webster, and Israel Baum married Lena Crohn. Some years after that, Abbe's daughter Leah became the wife of Theodore Crohn. Thus began what my father's relatives referred to as the "Baum-Webster Family Tree," which over the years, after generations of children, grandchildren and unions with new family groups, developed so many limbs and branches that it required the skills of a demographer to reconstruct.

In order to support his growing family, Abbe now went into the real estate business. The lower East Side was, at the time, a vibrant, growing community where nearly all of New York's approximately 12,000 Jews lived, most of them newly-arrived immigrants from Eastern Europe. What is now 42nd Street was then "uptown," some of it still farmland. Abbe's children later recalled being sent there by their father on the Passover holiday to buy fresh milk.

Admired and respected for his piety, erudition and honesty, Abbe soon became a leader in the community. As was the custom in those days, he took many of the newly arrived Jewish immigrants fresh off the boats into his home on East Broadway, where they were fed, furnished with clothing and helped in finding a job. At a later date he was appointed by the Mayor of New York to a committee to welcome the new arrivals from Europe, who at that time landed at Castle Garden, at the foot of the Battery. When the city's first synagogue, the so-called Great Synagogue, was opened in 1852, Abbe was one of its founders. In that same year the "Jews Hospital" (later named "Mt. Sinai Hospital") was founded by German and Spanish-Portuguese Jews, and located in a rented brownstone house on West 28th Street.

In 1853 when P.T. Barnum brought over Jennie Lind, the "Swedish Nightingale," from Europe, to sing at the Crystal Palace on the site of what is now Bryant Park, behind the public library, Abbe took his young wife, Goldie, to hear her. In order to get there from downtown on East Broadway, they were obliged to take a horse-drawn trolley to 14th Street, and a horse and buggy from there to 42nd Street.

When the Civil War started, the Baum brothers and their Webster relatives, who already had growing families to support, were allowed, like thousands of others, to hire for $300 young volunteers to serve in the army in their place. The family witnessed the draft riots of 1863 in Central Park, and Abbe's daughter Leah, then a child, later recalled seeing Negroes hung from street lamp posts. The family's colored seamstress was hidden by Abbe in the cellar of their house on East Broadway. Leah, a little girl in hoop skirts, stood on a barrel on a street of the lower East Side and witnessed the funeral cortege of Abraham Lincoln winding its way through the city.

Toward the end of the Civil War or shortly thereafter, the brothers embarked on one more adventure that they hoped would make their fortunes. The first successful oil well had been drilled in Western Pennsylvania. Abbe and Israel together with their brothers-in-law "Yank" Webster and Theodore and Marcus Crohn set out for Titusville, Pennsylvania, where they opened up a small store and eventually acquired the ownership of a small oil well. However, according to the family chronicle, when a representative of John D. Rockefeller, who had extensive oil properties in the vicinity, offered to buy them out and they refused, their "gusher" fell silent. Apparently Mr. Rockefeller's agents had drilled a series of wells around the periphery of their property and, in effect, siphoned off their well, which went dry.

As his family grew and his financial circumstances improved, Abbe moved from the lower East Side, initially to the north Bronx, thereafter to what is now Harlem, and eventually, in 1879, to a house on 85th Street and Madison Avenue. Wherever the family went, Abbe managed to keep his religious way of life and orthodox Jewish traditions. His grandchildren recalled that when they visited their grandfather at his home in the West Farms-Tremont area of the Bronx, which was then largely farm country, they were obliged to take the Third Avenue elevated train to the end of the line at 177th Street, where, if they were not met by grandpa's horse-drawn carriage, they had to trudge for miles across open fields to the Baum home. Since there were few Jews in the Bronx, whenever a "minyan" (the ten Jews necessary to be present before religious services could be held—boys under thirteen didn't count) could not be rounded up in his area, Abbe had to walk for miles to the Lebanon Hospital on East 149th Street to find a few of his co-religionists for Sabbath and holiday services.

When the family moved to their new home on 85th Street, Abbe's Jewish neighbors met initially at his home for prayers, and later at a small synagogue which they built on 82nd Street. Abbe had a beautiful voice, and it was the custom for him as honorary cantor to chant the opening Kol Nidre prayer on the eve of the Day of Atonement, as well as the concluding service on the following day. So impressive was his rendition of these rituals, that some people from the lower East Side walked all the way up to the 82nd Street Synagogue to hear him.

Abbe never became rich. There are numerous family stories of the real estate deals that he almost made, of the properties that he "could have bought" but didn't,

Abbe and Goldie Baum

such as the land where R.H. Macy's department store now stands. But he and his wife Goldie managed to bring up a family of ten children, most of whom went to college and on to the professions of law, medicine and teaching, all of them working to pay for their schooling and contributing to the support of the household. It was a happy, joyous family, a haven of warm hospitality. The Jewish holidays were great occasions. Lawrence Crohn recalled his grandmother Goldie Baum, a small simple woman, dressed in her holiday attire, "a black taffeta dress with an antique brooch at her lace collar. On her head she wore a small oval doily of real duchess lace, in the center of which was a small lavender velvet bow. She wore, in addition, exquisite pear-shaped opal earrings and a ring, in diamond frames."

Another grandson, Dr. Burrill Crohn, had this to say about his Baum-Webster-Crohn progenitors:

"Life in this country was good; the families prospered moderately. The spirit of devout religion permeated the home. The synagogue was their sanctuary; education counted more than wealth, which was not sought after and rarely attained. Geniality, culture, intelligence, friendliness, and philanthropy were their ideals. They were people who loved each other, who were happy in being sympathetic, wholesome and charitable. But they were also a hardy lot and adventurous, with a wanderlust that drove them to seek the pot of gold that lay beyond the rainbow, and that's where it stayed!"

Abbe never forgot or diminished his concern for the poor and unfortunate. His grandchildren remember him wearing his stove-pipe silk hat on weekdays, as he set out to make his calls on the poor. He died in 1902 at the age of 74. The doors of the 82nd Street Synagogue were opened in his honor as the funeral cortege passed by, with hundreds of community leaders and ordinary citizens walking behind the coffin.

Abbe had ten children, seven daughters and three sons. One son, David, became a lawyer, and another, Joseph, a physician who, as "Doc Baum"–a huge, jovial man weighing nearly three hundred pounds–was a familiar and popular figure in the Rockaways. Another daughter, Leah, married to Theodore Crohn, raised with him a colorful brood of a dozen children, which became the Crohn branch of the Family Tree. Since in those days teaching school was often the only prospect of employment for young educated women, four other daughters–Rebecca, Sarah, Millicent and Mallie–all taught school, with Millicent and Mallie making it their lifetime careers. Sarah, a person of enormous energy and dynamism, married Edward Epstein and started still another offshoot of the family.

Esther

My grandmother Esther, the oldest of Abbe's children, who married Samuel S. Ruskay, was cultured, highly intelligent and well-read. She was a gifted writer, an accomplished musician and a formidable public speaker, the first woman to speak from the pulpit of Temple Emmanuel–then at 42nd Street and Fifth Avenue. Her articles on Jewish life appeared in numerous newspapers, and a collection of her writings, called *Hearth and Home Essays*, was published in 1902 by the

Jewish Publication Society. She loved the piano and on returning home from the opera would regale the family by playing by ear some of the arias she had just heard. Intensely involved in Jewish affairs, she was one of the founders of the New York section of the Council of Jewish Women, the Educational Alliance and the Young Women's Hebrew Association, among other organizations. She numbered among her friends Professor Solomon Schecter, Dr. Joseph Mayer Asher, Mordecai Kaplan, Mrs. Alexander Kohut, Judge Samuel Greenbaum, Louis Lipsky and other well-known figures in the American Jewish community.

In 1884 there was a heated ongoing debate in the press and on the pulpits of Jewish houses of worship. On the one hand there were the supporters of Reform Judaism who urged the relaxation and reformation of Orthodox Jewish religious observance, including the reduction and deemphasis of Hebrew in synagogue services and Jewish education—as part of an effort to integrate American Jews, and especially the thousands of newly arriving immigrants from Eastern Europe, into the mainstream of modern American life. Most Jewish leaders adopted this stand. On the other hand there were those who insisted that there was no need for patriotic American Jews to give up their immemorial traditions, religious observances and Jewish identity. Esther J. Ruskay was a fervent advocate of the latter point of view, which she voiced in a speech on the subject, "The Revival of Judaism," delivered before the Council of Jewish Women on May 9. 1884. Her nephew, Lawrence Crohn, cited the following excerpts from the speech as illustrating "the eloquent style and profound feeling of our Aunt Esther":

> "Before starting to write my paper, I looked up the definition of 'revival' and found it to mean a return to life, an awakening. Clearly then Judaism was either dead or sleeping and needed to be awakened; and to me was deputed the task. I did not look up the word 'Judaism.' I thought I knew what this meant, and if I did not, there was no danger of my remaining unenlightened. In my experience, I have had served up to me splendid specimens of the accepted vernacular of modern Judaism, such as the 'essence of Judaism,' 'rationalistic,' 'universal spirit of Judaism,' all as pat and neatly rounded off into sentences as any orator ever succeeded in launching forth from the pulpit.
>
> I am not sure that I shall succeed in the 'awakening' part of my mission, but I am sure I shall arouse discussion and criticism, perhaps even censure and scorn.
>
> Hebrew among Jews is their universal shibboleth. Go where you will from East to West, from pole to pole, everywhere you find in some out-of-the-way corner of the globe, a band of men closely united. In the heart of Asia, in the wilds of Africa, on the plateaus of Mexico the 'Shema Yisroel' discovers a brother at your side, and is as sweet to the ear as the sound of running water to the thirsty traveler in the desert."

Esther's husband, my grandfather Samuel S. Ruskay, was a Wall Street broker. A handsome man, tall and slender with a carefully trimmed mustache and beard, always elegantly dressed, he was a great favorite with the ladies and notoriously unfaithful to my grandmother. Although he professed to be a confidante of prominent and wealthy figures in the financial world, his fortunes gyrated precariously as did the family style. For a while the Ruskays lived almost penuriously in the further reaches of the Bronx in Tremont, largely surrounded by

Esther J. Ruskay

farmland. Later, when Samuel's fortunes improved, they moved to a house on 86th Street and Second Avenue. However the family's finances ebbed and flowed, Esther saw to it that her three sons Burrill, Everett and Cecil, all went to college. Burrill eventually joined his father in Wall Street. Everett and Cecil became lawyers and, for a while, practiced as partners.

Everett, in addition, was a talented and successful playwright, the author of a number of successful plays, musicals, and vaudeville sketches, including "The Meanest Man in the World," which was produced by George M. Cohan, with Alan Dinehart in the leading role. A member of the Friar's Club, Everett was well-known in theatrical circles as the result of which the brothers for a while numbered many actors and vaudevillians among their clients. He was always a big hit at family gatherings and parties, where his scintillating wit and dry humor evoked howls of laughter. A popular man about town and extremely attractive to women, he nevertheless, like his brother Burrill, remained the perennial bachelor, although he liked to tease his mother by threatening to marry "outside the faith." Tragically, he died at the early age of 37.

In those days, around the turn of the century, many New York Jewish families sought to escape the city's summer heat at the Jersey shore, or at Arverne or Edgemere in the Rockaways. Some of the more affluent, like my mother's family, the Liebowitzes, built elaborate mansions near the beach at Arverne. During one of those periods when their finances were at a low ebb, the Ruskays, unable to afford renting even a modest conventional cottage, persuaded Remington Vernon, a wealthy owner of beach front property at Edgemere, to allow them and a number of other hardy families to start a small tent colony on the beach bordering his property. Arrangements were made to transport beds, tables, chairs, dressers and other furniture down from the city. The Ruskay sons erected a large platform tent as living quarters, a smaller tent for cooking, an outhouse, and dug a well for water. The tent for Esther and the family had a rug on the floor, Indian prints on the divans, a brass oil lamp on a table covered with a cashmere shawl, and even a small battered piano.

One of our family's treasured bits of memorabilia (now unfortunately lost) was a photograph of Grandma Esther, fully dressed in the cumbersome clothing of that period, sitting at a small table at the front opening of her tent, busily writing; while behind her, dimly visible, are all the accoutrements of a modest family household. It was here that during those summers she did her writing, carried on her correspondence, and received her visitors from the city, including prominent members of the intelligentsia and leading figures in Jewish affairs. Sad to say, this great lady was stricken suddenly with a brain tumor and died at the age of 43.

Courtship and Marriage

It was here too on the beach at Edgemere that one summer day my father's cousin, Burrill Crohn, introduced him to my mother Sophie, the only daughter of the well-to-do Simon and Fanny Liebowitz, the owners of a large shirt and pajama manufacturing business, who occupied a large house in nearby Arverne. Sophie, only eighteen at the time, was in her first year at Barnard College and Cecil, twenty-one, was attending law school while holding down a part-time job as desk clerk at a New York hotel. A great talker like his mother, Cecil charmed Sophie with his knowledge and enthusiasm for literature. They would meet and walk together on the beach early in the morning, before Cecil had to catch a train for the city; and Cecil would read extracts from a pocket volume of English Romantic poets or recite passages from Shakespeare. They were soon deeply in love.

For weeks they managed to keep their friendship a secret from Sophie's family. When eventually Fanny discovered the reason why her daughter had been getting up at dawn to stroll on the beach, she was furious. While the Liebowitzes had great respect for Esther Ruskay and the Baum family, the idea of her Sophie marrying a young man who was just finishing law school and whose financial prospects were dubious at best, was out of the question. Her parents and older brothers talked to Sophie and tried to reason with her and, as the months passed, they thought that they had convinced her.

But the young couple were not easily discouraged. Their courtship had all the melodrama of the dime novels so popular at the time. Barred of course from visiting the Liebowitz home, Cecil met Sophie secretly at libraries, museums and in Central Park. They dispatched letters and messages to one another through one of Cecil's cousins or other intermediaries. Inevitably they were found out and Fanny threatened dire consequences. Sophie wept, fell ill and took to her room. Her parents became alarmed. As a last resort, Sophie's uncle, the redoubtable and highly respected Israel Unterberg, was summoned to talk to his niece in a final effort to bring her to her senses. All to no avail. In the end, Fanny gave in and Love triumphed. They were married a year later, shortly after Cecil graduated from law school and had opened a small law office with his brother Everett in the Flatiron Building.

My father liked to tell this story about himself: Shortly after he was married, he was riding one morning in a Broadway streetcar, reading his newspaper on the way downtown to his law office. He had only recently passed the bar, and didn't have his first client yet–much less his first law case. On the seat next to him was an elderly Jew who insisted on striking up a conversation.

"What's your name, young man?"

"Cecil Ruskay," my father replied and went back to reading his paper.

After a few moments of silence, his neighbor interrupted him again.

"And what do you do?" he asked.

"I'm a lawyer," my father said and resumed reading.

"So you're a lawyer," the old man went on in disbelief as he appraised my father with obvious skepticism.

More resolutely than ever, Cecil buried himself in his newspaper. But the old man was not to be disposed of so easily. After a minute he turned to Cecil again.

"Married? Are you married?"

"Yes I am," Cecil said impatiently.

"And who is the fortunate bride?" his neighbor continued.

"Sophie Liebowitz. I married Sophie Liebowitz and we live on Pinson Place in Far Rockaway." And with that Cecil turned away from his companion and gave his newspaper a defiant shake to signal that the conversation was at an end.

There was a minute or two of silence while the old man closed his eyes and kept muttering to himself: "Liebowitz . . . Liebowitz? . . . Liebowitz?" Then he turned to my father once more and asked,

"Not the daughter of Simon Liebowitz, the shirt people?"

"Yes," Cecil replied, "she's the daughter of Simon Liebowitz."

At that the old man nudged Cecil in the ribs, smiled broadly and whispered in a conspiratorial tone, "She's ugly, huh?"

In fact, Sophie was a very attractive young woman. A charcoal portrait of her made by a young German artist in 1921, during a trip to Europe with Cecil, reveals an almost classic profile–a slightly arched Roman nose, dark eyes, purposeful mouth and chin, a long graceful neck and shoulders. Indeed some ten years later when I was twenty-one and my mother and I met in England for a walking trip to Yorkshire, the landlady of a small country inn took us for brother and sister, and was astonished when I told her that my walking companion was my mother.

Shortly after their first child was born, the Ruskays decided to move to Far Rockaway which, for years, had been a popular summer resort but was now a thriving year-round community. Though actually within the borders of New York City, Far Rockaway still possessed many of the characteristics of a small country town. Milk (Bordens and Sheffield), ice and about everything else was delivered by horse-drawn wagons–or sleighs in the middle of winter. Only the very rich owned automobiles. We walked!–to synagogue, to the village, to the beach, and back. The population was predominantly Protestant and Roman Catholic, but the Jewish community was

Sophie Ruskay

growing rapidly. People were friendly and neighborly. Everyone seemed to know everyone else. Apart from the local merchants, the business professional and other working people commuted to the city via the Long Island Railroad.

Pinson Place where we lived was only three or four blocks from the village and the railroad station. At the end of the block was a large twenty-acre farm where every year when it was in town, the Sparks circus set up its show tents, wild animal cages, freak show and other facilities. One of my earliest childhood memories is being taken by my older sister one day when the circus was in town to the fence bordering this farm, and staring, bug-eyed, at a family of American Indians–father, mother and children–part of the circus's Wild West show, dressed in their native regalia, sitting in front of their wigwam, eating their midday meal. Little did they know, as I was to discover years later, that, less than half-a-mile away, where Pinson Place ended at the inlet of Jamaica Bay, there were clearly visible traces of the flattened shards of clam and oyster shells that marked the trails, which three hundred or so years earlier, the local Indian tribe had trod in the course of their hunting and fishing activities. It was this tribe, the Rockaways, which before they were driven out by the early settlers, gave its name to the region which now stretches from Hammels to Woodmere.

In the summer, especially on weekends, every family went down to the ocean, either to Ostend or Roache's Beach, to swim, picnic and lie in the sun. Everything was very simple and unpretentious. There were no swimming pools or fancy private beach clubs. An open-air trolley car clattered on a single track from the railroad station down Central Avenue through the village to the beach. You just stepped on the running-board, even if the trolley was in motion, and climbed in. The fare was a nickel.

There being no synagogue in town, observant Jewish families held their Sabbath and holiday services in a rented store. But as the Jewish population grew, funds were raised and the Shaaray Tefilah Synagogue was built. Cecil was one of its founders and original trustees. The first rabbi was a young man from Pittsburgh named Lichter, and since the congregation could not afford to provide him with a home, he was taken in as a boarder by my great-uncle, the popular Doctor Joseph Baum, still a bachelor who lived alone with his mother Goldie, the widow of Abbe Baum.

My parents were soon deeply involved in local affairs. Sophie became active in the Sisterhood at the synagogue and in the local chapters of Hadassah and the National Council of Jewish Women. She dressed well but simply, setting no great store on her clothes or her appearance. She was far too busy with her community activities, not to mention the responsibilities of running a household and bringing up a family of five children. Nor did she stand on ceremony when her assistance was needed for the more mundane domestic chores. More than once I recall seeing her, with Margaret, her hard working maid-cook from Barbados, the two of them on their hands and knees scrubbing the kitchen floor, or cleaning the old-fashioned iron stove.

Cecil

Meanwhile, my father was in New York City every day, practicing law with his brother Everett. After the untimely death of Everett, Cecil became a partner in the firm of Miller, Bretzfelder and Ruskay. The senior partner was Cyrus Miller, a politician and former borough president of the Bronx. Bretzfelder was a well-connected resident of Westchester with a substantial clientele. Cecil, the youngest partner, did most of the firm's court work and rapidly became a skillful trial lawyer. His pleasant personality and ease of manner, not to mention occasional displays of his sense of humor, made him a favorite with judges and juries. Years later during a brief period when I served as his law clerk, I recall an instance that was typical of his courtroom aplomb. He was trying an important personal injury case that lasted several days. It was my job to get to the court early each day and "hold" the case until Cecil arrived. On the third day of the trial I was in the courtroom at 10 A.M., the case was called and Cecil, who had traveled by train and subway from his home in Lawrence, Long Island, was late. The judge was on the bench, members of the jury were in their seats. The former was furious, the latter restless. I kept looking anxiously at the clock and the courtroom door. Finally, at 10:30, Cecil made his appearance, approached the bench a bit out of breath but smiling, and proceeded to recount his misadventures and the shortcomings of the Long Island Railroad with such grace and humor that His Honor, the members of the jury and even opposing counsel were soon smiling.

Another time he was trying an estate fraud case in the Manhattan Surrogate's Court when that court was presided over by those two great jurists, Surrogates O'Brien and Delehanty, both of whom, though they were believed to have attained their positions through Tammany Hall, ran their court according to the strictest, most exacting standards of propriety and integrity. Judge Delehanty, who was hearing Cecil's lawsuit, was known to be especially severe. It was rumored that no one had ever heard him laugh. In the course of urging the court to admit a crucial piece of evidence, Cecil illustrated his argument with a tale of two perpetually feuding Irishmen, one from Kerry and the other from Cork–one of my father's better stories–at the conclusion of which the whole courtroom burst out laughing. From where I happened to be sitting, I was able to observe on the face of the judge as he turned his back to the courtroom in his swivel chair, the faint smile which he was unable to suppress. Then he turned around again, overruled the objection and admitted the evidence.

At the Inwood Country Golf Club, which he joined to attract new clients, Cecil soon became well known for his story telling. So called "dirty jokes," however, were not in his repertoire. Good at imitating Irish, Italian, Jewish and other accents, his brand of humor usually revolved around the comic frailties, shortcomings and idiosyncrasies of human nature.

He was also a capable public speaker. In those days before television and when popular radio broadcasts were still in their infancy, community forums and lectures featuring prominent public figures were the fashion, especially in suburban areas. As chairman of

The Progress Society of the Rockaways, which met once a month at the Masonic Temple, Cecil had the job of introducing the speaker of the evening. It was also customary for the chairman to entertain the evening's lecturer at his home for dinner preceding the meeting. On one such occasion the speaker who was our dinner guest turned out to be Admiral Peary, the discoverer of the North Pole. After the meal and before we all left for the meeting hall, the admiral was ushered into the living room for an after-dinner cigar and I, then a small boy, was invited to sit on the great man's lap. Several weeks later, as a gesture of appreciation for a pleasant evening at our home, a gift arrived–a framed photograph of the admiral together with a second picture, entitled "Peary's ship, the S.S. Roosevelt, fighting her way North"; and below them, an inscription: "To Joseph A. Ruskay," signed "Robert E. Peary."

However, these dinners and post-prandial entertainments of the guest lecturer didn't always turn out so pleasantly. One evening the speaker was W.E.B. Dubois, the famous black scholar and writer, and outspoken critic of white society thirty years before the civil rights movement was born, in whose eyes the leaders of the National Association of Colored People were a bunch of "Uncle Toms." Unfortunately, Sophie had been so unwise as to also invite for dinner a few close friends, including Mr. and Mrs. George Katz. Mr. Katz, the head of a large and very successful advertising agency, was a charming, courteous gentleman of the Old School, a man with very positive views on every subject, all of them extremely conservative, which he never hesitated to express. Sure enough, after dinner George took exception to one of Mr. Dubois' remarks about racial intolerance, and a furious argument broke out. Only Cecil's considerable diplomatic skills averted a total disaster.

Cecil also wrote poetry, most of it in the form of sonnets to Sophie, preserved by the family in a small volume printed privately years ago. True, it was not great poetry, somewhat old-fashioned and derivative. Still the verses are full of warm sentiments, deeply even passionately felt, and are often quite charming. What else? He also sketched and painted. However, he didn't really know how to draw; knew nothing of anatomy and the human figure. Furthermore, egoist that he was, he refused to take lessons, although he had a number of friends and clients who were skilled artists and who would have been only too glad to teach him. Consequently, his subjects were usually landscapes. Still clients, friends and relatives to whom he gave his pictures and drawings cherished them as warmly as if they were masterpieces–because they came from Cecil, who they admired.

However, he had one talent which was truly unique–the ability to take in his hand a play, be it a tragedy of O'Neill or a comedy of Shakespeare, and reading from it, create for his audience a sort of one-man theater. Whether it was on a platform at Columbia College or Cooper Union, or at an intimate gathering in his own living room, he had the extraordinary gift of being able to communicate a sense of theater to groups of people, whether they were sophisticated college graduates or ordinary workmen who had never been to a theater in their lives. All alone, without a single prop, taking all the roles, often of characters speaking in a variety of dialects, he was able to make the whole thing almost as dramatic, vivid and real is if it was being performed by a group of actors on a stage.

Once a year, Everett Dean Martin, its executive director, would invite Cecil to perform one of his dramatic readings at Cooper Union in downtown New York City, where the audience included many ordinary people with little or no education, let alone knowledge of the theater, many of them unemployed who left the streets for the auditorium because it was warm and the performance was free. On such occasions Cecil, usually choosing from his repertoire something with maximum dramatic effect, such as O'Neill's *The Hairy Ape*, or O'Casey's *The Plough and the Stars*, would hold his audience spellbound. But at other times he did not hesitate to do portions of *Hamlet* or *Macbeth*, even for working-class audiences.

One summer, when Sophie and Cecil were visiting me at Camp Modin in Maine, where I was a camper, the camp's directors, who knew my parents well, asked Cecil to give one of his dramatic readings for the camp's Saturday evening entertainment. He chose Lord Dunsany's *A Night at the Inn*, a fantastic play about a gigantic idol that mysteriously appears at an old inn in an English seaport town, to wreak a grisly vengeance on a group of Cockney sailors who, on their last voyage to India had stolen from its head, the idol's single eye made of precious diamonds. The entire camp, including youngsters of five and six, counselors and visiting parents, were assembled in the darkened social hall where, as if to make the setting still more sinister, Cecil stood at a small table on the stage with only a single candle for a light; and outside, nature added to the dramatic atmosphere by providing a summer storm with occasional rolls of thunder and flashes of lightning. The climax of the play comes when the huge idol starts to climb the stairs to the upper room where the three thieves are celebrating their exploit with a drunken orgy, and discussing the sale and division of the spoils. As the huge idol mounts the stairs slowly, one by one, Cecil pounded the table with his fist, louder and louder. Finally, as the sailors shriek with terror, the monster bursts into the room, crushes them to death one by one, seizes its stolen eye, claps it back in place in its head, and thunders back down the stairs. After the performance the campers returned to their tents and bunks, but it was some time before the counselors of the youngest children were able to induce them to go to sleep.

Life at the Ruskay Home

Life in the Ruskay home, although sometimes a bit hectic, was a happy and full one. Cecil and Sophie with their interest in theater, music and good literature, and their involvement in community affairs set a solid example for their children. Education, intelligence and culture were important. Congeniality and friendliness were equally so.

On Friday evenings, the reading of a play by Cecil was a ritual. The living room would be crowded with family and invited friends, the younger people sitting or sprawling on the floor. Invariably there was a delay before the performance could begin because my father would refuse to start until Sophie was present. "Where is Sophie?" Cecil would shout. The answer was Sophie was busy helping to clean up in the kitchen, or upstairs on the telephone discussing last-minute arrangements connected with one of her numerous activities. Finally, she would make her appearance, smiling sheepishly, and the performance could start. Often, when a play–especially one of Shakespeare's–would go on until almost past midnight, one of the youngsters in the audience would grow restless and complain that it was too long. "Too long?" Cecil would reply; and then quoting Hamlet's words to Polonius in response to a similar complaint in the great scene with the players, he would add, "It shall to the barber's with your beard!"

On Saturday mornings and Jewish holidays, the family went to synagogue at Shaaray Telifah. But after lunch, my father would slip away to the Inwood Golf Club, not necessarily to play golf, but just as often to gamble and play cards with his friends for what we feared were rather high stakes. Strange that this gifted man, a lover of good books and music, the composer of tender sonnets to his wife, possessed also a weakness for gambling, probably a heritage from his father Samuel, the Wall Street broker. Sophie would gently take him to task about this, but he would put her off with a smile and a joke. We never knew how much of the family fortune was frittered away at the card table on those Saturday afternoons.

Saturday afternoon was also the occasions for the weekly visit by Sophie's parents, Fanny and Grandpa

Simon Liebowitz, who would drive down in their car from the city with their chauffeur, Kennedy. Cecil's absence was explained by Sophie on the ground that the Inwood Club was where Cecil met important clients.

Fanny was an imposing woman, physically and otherwise. She towered over her husband who seemed meek and self-effacing by comparison. During the week she kept a sharp eye on the family shirt business. Every day she would be driven downtown by Kennedy to Leonard Street to see how her three older sons were running things. When she would arrive there early in the afternoon, the clerks, secretaries and other employees would bend their heads assiduously to their tasks, lest she catch them idling.

Although most people found her intimidating, forbidding even, the fact was she had a softer side, as I would discover as I grew older. She presided over the Ladies Fuel and Aid Society and other charities that distributed food, fuel, clothing and other necessities to poor Jewish families, and she was particularly fond of her many grandchildren.

However, she had no use or sympathy for "loafers," a category which in her mind included all of her husband Simon's "poor relations"–an assortment of sisters, uncles, aunts and their progeny, most of them elderly, unemployed, impoverished and speaking little or no English, who lived in the most distant parts of Brooklyn. For each of them Simon provided periodically modest financial support, a fact of which he sought to keep Fanny in ignorance. The secret agent, emissary and contact between Simon and these poor souls was Sophie, who faithfully and regularly traveled by railroad and

Fanny Liebowitz

subway to visit them, bringing not only money, but compassion and understanding.

And so it would happen, during these Saturday afternoon visits by my grandparents, that while Fanny was upstairs occupied with the younger grandchildren, Sophie would quietly slip away and join Simon, who would usually be sitting outside on the porch enjoying the sunshine. Then whispering together like two conspirators, Sophie would tell her father about her latest visits to his relatives in Brooklyn–to Aunt Sadie, Aunt Jennie, Uncle Morris and the others; and Simon would unobtrusively slip a handful of bills to his daughter, to be delivered by her on her next visit.

Visits to the City and the Theater

When we were very young, we were occasionally taken by our parents to visit our other grandfather, Samuel S. Ruskay, Cecil's father. After the death of his wife Esther, "S.S.," as he was known, gave up the family home on 86th Street and moved into a lavish apartment, complete with Japanese butler, where he lived with my Uncle Burrill, who had joined him in his stock brokerage business. There the old Wall Street buccaneer, charming and courtly as ever, rode the crest of the stock market boom until the collapse of his firm in the crash of 1929. But at this time he was riding high, brimming with confidence, the perfect host; and after our visit, he would take us "hicks" for a taxicab ride down Broadway to see "the Great White Way."

Although occasionally a first-rate chamber music group like the Clarence Adler Quartet would come down from the city to give a concert in the Rockaways, by and large the only local entertainment was the movies. But for hardy people like the Ruskays, New York City's theaters, the Metropolitan Opera and the concerts of the Philharmonic Orchestra were easily accessible, less than an hour's train ride on the Long Island Railroad. Regular subscribers to the Opera, the Philharmonic and the Theater Guild, Cecil and Sophie seemed to be in the city to attend a play or to hear music almost every week. There was one problem, however. In order to get home at a reasonable hour, they had to catch the 11:30 P.M. train at Penn Station. (The next train for the Rockaways didn't leave until an hour later). The result was that during the last–and often the most exciting–moments of a play, an opera or a concert, they had one eye on the clock, ready to dash madly, often on foot if no taxi was available, those dozen blocks to the railroad station. Sometimes they didn't make it.

They often took me and my older sister along with them to the theater, while we were still in our teens. It never occurred to Cecil or Sophie that the play we were about to see was one that most parents would consider utterly unsuitable for children our age; or if it did, they felt that our exposure to it could only be beneficial. I was only fifteen when I was taken to the lovely old Empire Theater to see a new play, translated from the French, which the City had tried, without success, to prevent from being shown. It was called *The Captive*, and concerned a beautiful married woman, a member of

Parisian society, who was a lesbian and led a double life. At the final curtain, resolved to resume her affair with her "lover" at all costs, she tells the butler as she leaves, to inform her husband that she will be gone for the evening. Such a subject had never even been mentioned before in a theater in this country.

Another time we were taken to see the Theater Guild's fine production of *The Brothers Karamazov*, with Alfred Lunt and Lynn Fontaine in the leading roles. In one torrid scene Lunt seized Miss Fontaine in his arms as she stood majestically center stage, and then covering her with passionate kisses, fondled her, traversing with his hands her entire body, starting at her throat, descending to her bosom, then to her stomach and thighs, while the audience gasped. No actors had ever dared to play a love scene like this before on a New York stage. My sister and I took it all in stride.

Sophie

People respected my father. They adored Sophie. A woman of enormous energy, she seemed to have time for everything and everyone. She soon rose to leadership positions in the community–president of Sisterhood at the synagogue, co-chair of the local board of Hadassah, coordinator of the annual fundraising drives for the Federation of Jewish Philanthropies. At the request of her friend Anna Cross, the New York City Commissioner of Correction, she conducted a class in drama for prisoners in the Women's House of Detention. A liberal in politics like her husband, in the late 1930s, after the family moved across the Nassau County line to Lawrence, she was persuaded to run for the State Assembly on the American Labor Party ticket, and ran a lively campaign, although doomed to defeat in that solidly Republican stronghold.

The Ruskays gave liberally to charity. But with Sophie giving to the established charitable organizations was not enough. She had what Cecil called "her projects," a list of poor and unfortunate people who had no one else to turn to–the plumber's wife, a chronic invalid to whom she would bring each week a boiled chicken and a pot of soup; her Italian laundress, who lived with her family of ten children "across the tracks" in Inwood and who was always in need of clothing, sheets, blankets and other necessaries; Mrs. Levy, a courageous little widow who managed to eke out a living operating a tiny grocery near the beach which Sophie insisted on patronizing, and several others that I no longer recall. When Sophie was too busy with other matters, I was the one usually deputized to go on these errands. This was before government welfare, home relief and social security.

In spite of all this activity, this remarkable woman somehow find time to write three books. On weekends and on vacations, while Cecil was at his easel, Sophie was scribbling away in her notebooks. Her first book, *Horsecars and Cobblestones*, a warm and gentle account of her years of growing up in New York City's lower East Side at the turn of the century, was highly praised by *The New York Times*, the *Saturday Review*, and other publications. *Discovery at Aspen*, a book for teenagers, retold the dramatic history of gold and silver mining in

Colorado during the last century, and the third, *The Jelly Woman*, was a collection of character sketches.

An attentive, loving daughter to her parents Fanny and Simon, she made it a point of keeping in touch regularly with her six brothers, their wives and children. She was particularly fond of the more outgoing and convivial relatives on my father's side of the family, with whom she was very popular. Whereas Cecil, especially if he had an appreciative audience, could be devastating, as he dissected the shortcomings of certain relatives, both on Sophie's and his own side of the family, with complete impartiality, Sophie saw these same uncles, aunts and cousins with different eyes, at once more gentle, tolerant and affectionate.

As a young girl, since her father Simon was always too tired at the end of the day to go out, preferring to stay home and read his newspaper, it was Sophie who would accompany her mother when Fanny wanted to go downtown at night to Second Avenue, to visit the Yiddish theater to see the great stars of the day–Jacob Adler, Bertha Kalisch, Morris Carnovsky and the rest–perform the classic melodramas and familiar comedies that were the lifeblood of the Yiddish stage. Now, years later, Sophie would occasionally take her mother along with us when we went to a play or concert. One night, I and two of my sisters, together with Sophie and Fanny took our seats in the fifth row of the orchestra at Carnegie Hall just before the expected chamber music concert was about to start. But instead of two violinists, a cellist and a viola player, onto the stage trooped forty young Russian singers–tenors, baritones and basses, brilliant in their native Cossack dress, boots and woolen caps, who burst into a beautiful Russian folk song. It was the internationally famous Don Cossack Chorus making its New York debut! Sophie had gotten the concert dates mixed up. Fanny, who had come to this country as a young girl from a small village in Eastern Europe shortly after our Civil War, remembered only too well the grandfathers of these young men as the dreaded troops of the Czar who slaughtered Jews and burned their villages in periodic pogroms. Rising abruptly from her seat, and unmindful of the discomfort and annoyance to her neighbors, she pushed her way angrily and unceremoniously toward the aisle and stormed out of the auditorium. There was nothing for us to do but to follow her. At a later time when they toured the country again, I was fortunate to be able to hear this wonderful group and their splendid renditions of Russian folk songs, and of traditional Greek Orthodox Church music.

Except for Sophie's fling at running for the New York State Assembly in the 1930s, my parents were not interested in politics. However, their strongly held views on current social problems and world events were bound to involve them from time to time in local controversies. In the 1920s, the Rockaways Jewish community was bitterly divided on the issue of Zionism, the proposal of a national home for uprooted Jews in Palestine. The majority, led by Rabbi Isaac Landman, the spiritual head of the Reformed Temple in Far Rockaway an editor of the antizionist publication *The American Hebrew*, felt that support for Zionism raised doubts about their American patriotism. Sophie and Cecil and other fervent Zionists rallied the community with public meetings and fundraising affairs, and their views eventually prevailed. Years later, the civil war in Spain and Russian War Relief during World War II again split the community with conservatives and most local Catholics charging that supporters of Loyalist Spain and of aid to Russia during the war were Communist dupes, or worse. Sophie and Cecil, prompted by their own children and other liberals and progressives in the area, became deeply involved, with Cecil being asked to take the chair at public meetings because of his calm platform manner and reputation for fairness. Invariably a contingent of angry, vociferous and often violence-prone locals would enter the auditorium and try to break up the meetings. However, Cecil's composure and a combination of firmness and geniality on his part usually prevented matters from getting out of hand.

To the Mountains

When my father and his cousin Burrill Crohn were both attending City College, they used to walk downtown together from 86th Street to Lexington Avenue and 23rd Street, where the college was located, and later walk back uptown again, in order to save the five cents carfare for their Saturday night poker games. That is perhaps where my father developed his taste for hiking. At any rate, as long as I can remember, my parents took their children, almost as soon as they could walk, to the mountains, first to the Catskills and later to the more challenging trails in the Adirondacks and White Mountains, to hike and climb. These family expeditions

Cecil B. Ruskay

were always great fun. Cecil usually managed to keep everyone's spirits up, although for him, a heavy man seriously overweight, climbing mountains could not have been easy. Still, he made light of his difficulties. In the middle of a particularly steep ascent, he would stop, remove his battered old hat, wipe the perspiration from his brow, look at the rise towering above him and exclaim, "Psalm of David: 'I will lift up mine eyes unto the mountains from whence cometh my help.'" Then, after a pause, he would add: "Whence cometh my help?"

I have another indelible picture of him. It is a hot, early September day in the Catskills. He is sitting, resting for a few moments beside a running mountain brook, his boots and stockings off, his pants rolled up with his feet in the cool water, and on his face a smile of pleasure and relief that one could only describe as beatific.

People who have never climbed the headwall of Tuckerman's Ravine on a hot summer day to reach the summit of Mount Washington, will not have had to endure the pain and agony that necessarily accompany it. But at the same time, they will never experience the exhilaration of attaining the top, of drinking in the clear mountain air, and of seeing the sun sink slowly below the surrounding peaks. I have my parents to thank for opening up this world to me.

He and Sophie were still climbing mountains whey they were well into their fifties. While in Mount Ranier National Park one summer, they learned there was to be a climb, led by professional guides, scheduled to ascend from the Paradise Inn at 5,000 feet to Camp Muir at the 10,000-foot level, where the climbers would spend the night in sleeping bags and descend the next day. Cecil suggested that they join the group and Sophie, with some misgivings, agreed. At 6:30 A.M. the next morning, the group of ten men and one woman, all in their twenties or early thirties, plus Sophie and Cecil, shepherded by two guides, had their picture taken together before they started out. Four hours later, while still struggling in the snow fields well below their destination, Sophie called a halt. Thoroughly exhausted herself, her chief concern was for Cecil, who was having difficulty breathing the thin mountain air and who she feared might have a heart attack. And so, accompanied by one of the guides and the other lady, who was also having problems, they slowly made their way back down. When at last they reached the Paradise Inn, the same photographer who had snapped the picture of the group before it had left that morning, was there to take another photo of Sophie and Cecil. The two pictures are a priceless family memento. In the first picture the two of them, outfitted like the rest with heavy sweaters and jackets, woolen hats, sturdy boots and thick climbing staffs, look fresh, bright and eager. In the second picture, drawn and haggard, their faces heavily lined and with dark shadows under their eyes, they are hardly recognizable. They looked like creatures out of Dante's Inferno.

The experience didn't discourage them, however. The next summer they were climbing in New Hampshire.

Cecil and Sophie at Mr. Rainier (before)

Sophie and Cecil at Mt. Rainier (after)

The Race for the 7:46 A.M. Train

After the family moved from Far Rockaway to New McNeil Avenue in Lawrence, just across the Nassau County border, the morning train of the Long Island Railroad, which Cecil formerly had boarded at Far Rockaway for the city, now had to be caught at the Inwood station, where it departed promptly at 7:46 A.M. However, since our new home was only ten or eleven blocks from the station, Cecil never allowed Sophie, who would be driving him to the train, to rush his breakfast, insisting always that there was time to spare. Finally, heeding his wife's frantic entreaties, he would get into the car and they would be off. But by this time the train, on its way from Far Rockaway, was already sounding its whistle for the Inwood crossing and it often happened that by the time they arrived, the train was already on its way.

Not to worry! There were still local stops up the line at Lawrence, Cedarhurst, Woodmere, Hewlett and Gibson, each of them only one or two miles apart, which the train was obliged to make before it started its express run to Jamaica and the city. So off Sophie would race, at Cecil's urging, up Central Avenue to the Lawrence Station. Too late again! So it went with the result that they would either catch up with the errant train at Hewlett or Gibson, or miss it altogether. Only then could Sophie, clad only in her nightgown with a coat or wrapper flung hastily over her shoulders, start for home and prepare for her customarily busy day.

Family Reunions and Parties

Every dozen years or so, my father's relatives, the Baum-Webster clan, now enlarged and enriched by Crohns, Epsteins, Zemans, Ruskays, Levines and several other offshoots, would have a family reunion in New York City. These were gay, festive affairs, usually held in a hotel ballroom, attended by as many as one hundred and fifty people, who came from all parts of the country. The high point of the evening was the entertainment, consisting of songs, verses and sketches, composed for the occasion, some of them funny and clever, others amateurish and silly, but all of them performed with relish and enthusiasm and warmly received. Bathroom humor was not only tolerated, it was applauded. Young children and sons-in-law and daughters-in-law attending one of these gatherings for the first time were required to participate in a mock-serious initiation ceremony, the "hupsy-clupsy," presided over by the Webster "boys," Bernie, Sidney and Leslie, three ageless, irrepressible jokesters who accompanied their slapstick verses, improvised on the spot, with a quite credible soft-shoe dance routine. This performance was always greeted with shrieks of laughter.

Later on in the evening, there would be a display of the family's erudition, sophistication and wit when, for example, Judith Epstein, the national president of Hadassah and a first-rate public speaker, rose to pay a moving tribute to the heritage and traditional values of the family and its contributions to the American Jewish community; or when Dr. Burrill Crohn, the celebrated gastroenterologist, the eldest son in a family of twelve children, delivered one of his inimitable descriptions of growing up in the Crohn household dominated by his fervently religious father.

On the other hand my mother's relatives, the Liebowitzes, never had any large family parties or reunions. Engrossed as they were in their growing shirt and pajama business, they didn't seem to have much time for frivolity or gaiety.

However, on Passover every year, we children were invited with our parents to Grandma Liebowitz's home on West 89th Street, for a seder attended by all her children and grandchildren. Just exploring this large house with its five floors was an adventure. We were fascinated by the library with its rows of glass enclosed bookcases, and formal front parlor, furnished in Victorian style, with antique chairs, tables, couches and cabinets, and with paintings and family photographs covering the satin damask walls. The seder itself was held in the large dining room in the rear of the second floor, which had a long carved oak table with matching upholstered chairs accommodating twenty-five or thirty people. The food was sent up from the kitchen in the floor below on a dumbwaiter, operated by hand ropes, and we were waited on by Grandma's two Irish maids in black dresses with white aprons and caps.

Unfortunately, the seder service itself was dull and disappointing. Grandpa and his older sons raced through the Haggadah in Hebrew, droning on and on in a monotone, with not a word left out, while we children waited impatiently for the food to be served. But the food, when it finally arrived, was marvelous–gefilte fish, hard-boiled eggs in salt water, and chicken soup with matzoh balls. And these were only the appetizers! However, the second half of the service, with its songs and riddles which is supposed to be more lively and informal, was no improvement; and the attempts of my father to introduce some of the more tuneful traditional melodies of the Baum-Webster seders, were not welcomed.

Mistakes and Disappointments

After five years as a partner in the growing, politically well-connected law firm of Miller, Bretzfelder and Ruskay, where his future as the firm's leading trial lawyer was assured, Cecil chose to leave that firm. Having acquired a number of important clients of his own, he decided to open up his own law office and become a businessman's lawyer. It was a grievous mistake. Cecil was no businessman. He soon found himself weighed down with the overhead of what, for those times, was a fair-sized law office, employing six lawyers, four secretaries and a clerk. The problems and responsibilities of the office diverted him from the phase of the law in which he excelled–trying cases before judges and juries, which he now did less frequently. His place was in the courtroom, and he never should have left it.

To make matters worse, his penchant for speculation, a legacy from his father, "S.S.," (and that was the only legacy that the former Wall Street broker left to his family!) led him to squander money on imprudent business ventures, and his investments in real estate were a family joke. There was the house in Sea Cliff on the North Shore of Long Island, that never seemed to attract a tenant, much less a buyer; and a charming little cottage in Arverne, that was a mile or more from the railroad station, and still further from the beach. Another investment in vast, unimproved acreage in Putnam County eventually had to be dropped. Finally, there was the house in Stony Brook, Long Island, ninety miles or so from the city, a veritable country estate with two acres of woodland, which Cecil acquired in lieu of fees for years of legal work, for Johnny Hyams the vaudevillian, the father of Leila Hyams the Hollywood actress. The only catch was this "gift" came encumbered with a hefty mortgage held by a local bank. Not knowing what else to do with this property, Sophie bravely attempted to make it our summer home for a number of years. Unfortunately, those of us who were working in Manhattan, including Cecil, were obliged to rise at dawn to catch the 6:50 A.M. Long Island Railroad train for the two-hour ride to the city. Another problem was clearing the place of leaves and brushwood that accumulated in stupendous quantities, especially in the fall. Since this required the work of many hands laboring days on end, the Ruskay children were encouraged to lure unsuspecting friends to come out and spend October and November weekends with us. Finally, during World War II when gas rationing made travel by auto to Stony Brook impossible, Cecil admitted defeat and allowed the bank to take over the property.

The fact was that Cecil's investments in real estate were in the Baum family tradition, with this difference: Whereas his great- grandfather Abbe Baum, as we have seen, "lost" money by failing to invest in real estate parcels which, had he done so, would have made his fortune, his great-grandson Cecil, on the other hand lost money by investing in properties that he should have avoided like the plague.

Worse still were his financial involvements with his brother, our Uncle Burrill, a kind, sweet, soft-spoken bachelor, and an incurable optimist who, after retiring from Wall Street, embarked on a series of business investments, each more hopelessly impractical than the others, and all destined to utter failure. Of two that I recall, the first was a dealership in specially-built, super deluxe foreign automobiles, Rolls Royces, Hispano Suizas, and others which were designed to be sold to the very wealthy. However, since the debut of this venture coincided with the depths of the 1930s Depression, it was not surprising that few cars were sold, and the dealership was short lived. Another project of Burrill's was the "Smokerset," nothing more or less than an attractive metal, box-like ash tray, the upper part of which would divide and open up when one depressed a lever or button, allowing the cigar or cigarette ash to fall to the bottom of the container, after which the two halves of the tray, activated by a simple spring mechanism, would close up again. Burrill and Cecil were so enthusiastic about this simple device that they spent a good deal of money trying to have it patented. Of course it proved to be unpatentable and the large inventory of "Smokersets" turned out to be unsaleable. To make matters still worse, the two brothers had persuaded several of Cecil's clients to invest in their brainchild.

An Unusually Happy Marriage

Still Cecil ("C.B.," as he was known to his family and friends), in spite of his financial concerns, never lost his composure or good humor. If he worried, and he often did, he didn't let on. He was a spender. When he bought a gift for Sophie, he would go to Tiffany's; and when his children dropped into his office, he would insist on taking them to the Biltmore or Roosevelt Hotel for lunch. As his oldest son, who inherited more of the Liebowitz trait of prudence with money than the Ruskay flair for extravagance, I frowned on all this improvidence. But my wife, who subscribed to the absurd notion that money should be spent and enjoyed, often teased me with the couplet, "Why can't you be,. more like C.B.?"

Sophie worried about her husband's hare-brained schemes with Burrill and would occasionally rebuke him on that account. But I doubt that they ever seriously quarreled. The only time I ever heard her lose her temper with him was when they were en route, by automobile, with the family to some destination in unfamiliar territory in northern Westchester or Connecticut, with Cecil at the wheel. When he got lost, as often happened, he would, in spite of Sophie's entreaties that he do so, stubbornly refuse to stop and ask for directions, persisting in adhering to his own trial-and-error method of navigation.

It was an unusually happy marriage. They both had a great zest for life. Though in many ways opposites–she a dynamo, he taking life as it came, or pretending to do so–their different temperaments meshed and complemented one another. Sophie was also tolerant and understanding in small ways. It always irked her, although she would laugh at it in retrospect, that she had to prod him to go to the Saturday night dances at the Inwood Club. He would just as well remain at home and paint or read out loud to her. But after he finally was persuaded to get dressed and go, he would invariably be the life of the party and thoroughly enjoy himself.

For all his outward poise and self assurance, Cecil was at bottom a very sentimental man. Very often, on holidays and other occasions when the whole family dined together, while leading the traditional grace after meals, he would look at Sophie and recite one of his favorite excerpts from another part of the prayer book–Proverbs XXXI:10-31:

"A woman of worth who can find? For her price is far above rubies. The heart of her husband trusteth in her; and he shall have no lack of gain. She doeth him good and not evil all the days of her life . . . Strength and majesty are her clothing, and she laughs at the time to come . . . She looketh well to the ways of her household and eateth not the bread of idleness. Her children rise up and call her happy, her husband also, and he praiseth her, saying: Many daughters have done worthily, but thou excellest them all . . ."

Then he would rise from his seat at the head of the table, go down to the other end and give Sophie a kiss. As he returned to his place, there were tears in his eyes that he was unable to hide.

But he was always careless about his health. He ate the wrong things, loved rich foods, thick soups and heavy sauces, insisting on adding salt to everything although he had a heart condition. As he approached his seventy-third birthday he became seriously ill, and Sophie fearing the worst, made arrangements for a family party in his honor at the Lawrence Village Golf Club. The family relatives, especially those on Cecil's side–the Baums, Crohns, Epsteins and the rest–came down from the city in large numbers. It was an impressive occasion, although somewhat on the somber side with so many of the old-timers no longer alive. There were speeches, songs, and toasts, serious and humorous, and although he looked quite feeble, Cecil roused himself for the occasion and was in fine form. Three months later he was on his deathbed.

Many years later at a noisy Bar Mitvah party for one of the younger members of the family, I found myself sitting alone at a table watching the young people dancing, reflecting somewhat moodily on the past. Suddenly, I was roused out of my stupor when Lara, a favorite great-niece of mine, quietly sat down beside me, laid her head on my shoulder and murmured:

"When first my heart awoke and found you there
Enthroned with love and joy on either side,
I scarce believed that unto me so rare
A gift would be entrusted to abide."

And then she continued to recite the rest of one of Cecil's earlier sonnets to Sophie. I almost broke down I was so moved by the fact that this lovely young woman, whose great-grandfather died before she was even born, having come across the little family volume of his poems, chose to commit one of them to memory.

Life After Cecil

Sophie was nearly seventy when Cecil died. She promptly sold the big New McNeil Avenue house and rented a two-and-a-half room apartment in the vicinity. There was never any thought of her living with one of her children; she was far too independent for that. She still had her automobile, which took her everywhere on her busy rounds. There were children and grandchildren scattered about the New York Metropolitan Area to be visited, not to mention others in Connecticut and the West Coast, Sophie keeping a watchful eye on the development of the youngsters, including giving them their first lessons in Hebrew. Added to this were trips to the city to pay calls on relatives, the rich ones and the poor ones, or for an occasional afternoon at a theater concert or museum. As if this were not enough, there was still the synagogue and meetings of the Sisterhood, Hadassah, Federation and other organizations in which she continued to be active. All of her life Sophie had been plagued with a sensitive stomach. Now her chronic indigestion was getting worse. Still the pace of her life slowed down little, if at all.

One year, out of the blue, she embarked on a five-week trip to Greece and Israel, taking with her her fifteen-year-old granddaughter Lynne, who later confessed that she had had difficulty keeping up with her grandmother. And years later, already in her eighties, unable to persuade any of her friends to accompany her, she toured the country alone on a Greyhound bus, from New York though the Southwest to California, stopping off at intervals to visit with friends and relatives.

For a small party celebrating her seventy-fifth birthday, I composed some doggerel satirizing a typical day in her frenetic life. It starts with a hurried visit to my home in nearby Woodmere, where Sophie proposed to store some possessions which she had no room for in her own apartment. My wife Margot, it turns out, is not at home. Sophie is greeted by her grandson David and a friend, and the following colloquy ensues:

Grandma, what are you doing here?
I've come to see your mother, dear.
She isn't home, she went to shop.
Then I'll leave these with you,
I've no time to stop.

What are those packages, Grandma, for?
They're just some things I want to store
Tell mother they go up on the third floor
And next week I'll be back with a dozen more.
When mother comes back, what shall I say,
Where are you going, Grandma, today?

Tell her I'm taking the 9:30 train
I have to visit the dentist again;
(And that reminds me, I must invite
The dentist's assistant to dinner some night).

From there, a visit to Jeannette May[1]
With a stop at my publisher's on the way,
Then over to Brooklyn–on the other hand,
I want to deliver that umbrella stand.

What umbrella stand, Grandma?

---

[1] A friend of Sophie's.

Well you see on the rear seat, that enormous thing
It's something I promised Aunt Libby I'd bring.
Tell Margot I've put it in the back of her car,
It's not out of the way, or so terribly far,
If she honks her horn to beat the band
The doorman may come and lend her a hand.
Where was I?–Oh yes.

From Jeannette's to Brooklyn, the connection is fine
By way of the Flatbush Avenue Line.
I want to pay a little call
On a relative I fear you don't know at all,
She's a poor little woman, all day alone
The wife of my cousin Maxie Cohen.
But what little tzatzki[2] can I bring?
Oh, that box of candy will be just the thing.
You children don't need it, it's awful to chew
It's bad for your teeth, and Deborah's too.
Grandma, tell me one thing more,
That paper parcel, what's it for?

Well it really isn't very much
Some hard boiled eggs and bread and such
Some nice cold tongue, I'm sure will do
And nicely serve as lunch for two.
We could get some coffee to go with that
And eat it at the Automat.

You see at half past one I have a date,
With the daughter of another cousin
And several friends, about half a dozen.
I promised to show them through a part
of the Metropolitan Museum of Art.
Perhaps there we'll find a spot to munch
Our tasty little bit of lunch

---

[2] An inexpensive gift.

In a quiet corner no one will mind
They say the guards are very kind.
But somehow I must contrive
To be at my brother Abe's by five
I promised to take him out for tea
It gives him a chance to talk to me.
And if there's time and on the way
I'll drag him over to see E.J.[3]
Then after that with little fuss
Abe's chauffeur will drive me to my bus.

What bus Grandma?

I forgot to say, at half past six
I'm on my way to visit Blix[4]
I go by Greyhound now and then,
It arrives at Wilkes Barre at half past ten;
The ride's not bad, at modest fare
Before I know it the bus is there.
Grandma, do you really mean to say
You're doing all of that today?

Well there are one or two things that I've left out
But they're nothing really worth worrying about.
On Friday morning, willy nilly
I leave for home by way of Philly,
I couldn't travel down that far
And not see how Lynne and Allen are.[5]
And I'll be back on Saturday night,
And get some rest, I'll be alright.
On Sunday I have guests for lunch

---

[3] Another brother of Sophie's.

[4] A daughter of Sophie's.

[5] A granddaughter and her husband.

Some lady friends, they're quite a bunch.
But I've got some chicken and split pea soup,
Enough to feed the entire group,
And Sunday evening, as we agreed,
I'm coming over to hear you read.
(She kisses David and leaves)
Said David's little friend from school
Your Grandma, David, is really cool.

Later Sophie started writing and producing little playlets for Hadassah, the National Council of Jewish Women and other organizations in connection with their fundraising activities. For inspiration, she drew on familiar Biblical themes–Esther, Mordecai and the Story of Purim, or that of Ruth and Naomi; or yet again, on dramatic events of recent history, such as the rescue of Jewish survivors of World War II and their escape via the underground to Israel. As performers she was able to recruit a dozen or more talented young married women, some of them with professional experience, all of them enthusiastic fans of Sophie. Simple, unpretentious, amateurish even though they were, these performances seemed to strike a sympathetic chord with local audiences, and as word of their success spread, the troupe was called upon to travel elsewhere in the Metropolitan Area and repeat them.

Sophie was also invited by these and other organizations to give "readings." On these occasions she would read excerpts and later discuss the works of contemporary writers–Bellow, Roth and Malamud were her favorites. Wherever she went and whatever the audience, she always brought with her a supply of her own *Horsecars and Cobblestones*, or one of her other books, having previously arranged with the meeting chairperson that the latter, at an appropriate time, would advise the audience that copies of one of Mrs. Ruskay's books could be purchased at the conclusion of the meeting. Sophie was not shy. She was her own best salesman.

Finally, when she was obliged to give up driving her car, Sophie moved to an apartment within walking distance of her synagogue. But getting around the Rockaways-Five Towns area now presented problems. More often than not her friends or members of her family were available to pick her up. Of course there were also taxicabs, but Sophie, generous in her gifts to charity and to others, was frugal when it came to spending on herself. Taxicabs? What for? They're hot, the drivers don't understand directions, they drive too fast, and so on. Her friends Naomi Joseph and Jeannette Gottlieb are better drivers; they have cars you can be comfortable in; you can roll down the window and get a breath of fresh air! When friends or family weren't available, she took the bus; and if the bus didn't come or she had just missed it, she was not above accepting a hitch from a total stranger. And why not? What was wrong with that? After all, the man had an empty front seat and was going in the same direction! Besides, you sometimes meet the most interesting people.

Eventually her increasingly painful arthritis required her to use a cane. Moreover, it became more and more evident that a twice-a-week household helper was inadequate, and that Sophie needed full-time, sleep-in care. So when she fell and fractured her hip, after a spell in the hospital she was persuaded to move into the King

David Manor, a hotel for elderly people in Long Beach. This was followed in the course of the next few years by a so-called health-related facility and eventually by nursing homes in Darien and West Hartford, Connecticut.

Still, Sophie didn't give up easily. Although she required first a walker, then a wheelchair, she fought the loss of her strength and mobility bravely, even fiercely, and persisted in a regular schedule of walking and exercise. She even gave "readings" to her elderly companions, though she must have been painfully aware that her audiences now were somewhat less eager and attentive than those she had been accustomed to in the past.

And strange to say, she still managed to retain something of her former vigor and youthfulness. Indeed, when her arthritis and rebellious stomach weren't making her too uncomfortable, or when she managed to forget them for a while, you might have seen her greet someone or start a conversation, perhaps with one of those elderly but still courteous gentlemen at the King David Manor, bestowing on her companion a flash of her old smile—warm, affectionate, almost coquettish.

Eventually however, the day came when, alone in her room at the West Hartford home, she suffered a stroke, fell and died without gaining consciousness. She was ninety-six years old.

Once again I glance at a photograph of my father's relatives—the Baum-Webster clan at a party held on April 17, 1913, at the Tuxedo Hotel in New York City, in honor of Mr. and Mrs. Jacob Webster, on the occasion of their fiftieth wedding anniversary. There they are, almost seventy of them–Baums, Websters, Crohns, Ruskays, Epsteins and the rest, the men in white ties, starched shirt fronts and tails–de rigeur for parties in those days–the ladies in elaborate formal gowns, all turned toward the photographer, some serious, others laughing. And among them, Cecil and Sophie, then a young married couple.

They are all gone now. But the photographer has caught them at this one moment of their lives, the elderly, proud and satisfied at what they have accomplished, the more youthful, eager, happy, smiling in anticipation of what life still has in store. And so shall they remain fixed in our memories.

Baum-Webster Clan Dinner (1913)

CHAPTER II

THE CROHN FAMILY

In March 1882 the relatives and friends of Abbe Baum in New York received the following written invitation:

"Mr. and Mrs. A. Baum request your presence at the marriage of their daughter Leah to Theodore Crohn, Wednesday evening March fifteenth at five o'clock at the residence of Mr. and Mrs. S.S. Ruskay, 109 East 116th St., New York."

Everyone knew Leah as the daughter of Abbe Baum, a highly respected figure in the New York Jewish community, one of the founders in 1852 of the Beth Hamidrash Hagodol, the Great Synagogue on Norfolk Street on the lower East Side, appointed by the Mayor as head of a committee to welcome new immigrants arriving from Europe. And Leah herself was admired for her marvelous lyric soprano voice and gentle charm. As a young woman she sang in the choir of Temple Emmanuel, then at 42nd Street and Fifth Avenue, on Saturdays and in St. Thomas' Church on Sundays, and was a member of the First New York Oratorio Society under the direction of Leopold Damrosch.

But who was this Theodore Crohn, the prospective bridegroom? It was known that, in 1849, as a boy of thirteen, he and his brother Marcus had come to America with their mother and sister, whom he helped support as an errand boy for a garment manufacturer for

$3 a week, and that his sister had married Israel Baum, Abbe's brother.

Beyond that his career as he described it was unusual to say the least. For a while the two Crohn brothers and Israel Baum had operated a general store in Titusville, Pennsylvania, and around 1870, after the discovery of silver in Colorado, the three left for the West. In Central City, Colorado, during the silver mining boom, the Crohn brothers together with a partner opened up a general merchandise store under the name of "Crohn Brothers and Hall, Temple of Fashion" and joined the local Masonic Lodge. Central City, while the silver boom lasted, was a wild, brawling town where gambling and drunkenness were everywhere and murder a common occurrence. Theodore became an expert pool player and on one occasion his life was saved by a fellow Mason when an angry drunkard whom he had beaten at the pool table threatened to kill him. A huge fire destroyed virtually everything in Central City, and the brothers lost everything, including their store, there being no insurance in those days. With the collapse of the silver boom, the Crohns made their way back East. The trip was made in a Wells Fargo stagecoach, with the brothers taking turns sitting on the roof alongside the driver with a shotgun across their knees to ward off attacks by Indians and outlaws. (Many years later, younger members of the family on a trip to Central City found the Crohn name still faintly visible on the side of an old building that had been their father's store).

Not long after returning to New York the brothers were summoned by their brother-in-law Israel Baum to Texas, where Israel and his relatives had established general stores in a number of small towns. Some time later on a trip to New York to buy merchandise, Theodore was invited to the home of Abbe Baum, where the young man fell under the spell of that friendly, pious man. He also met Abbe's daughter Leah and fell in love with her.

By any normal conventional standard this was surely a most unusual union. Theodore had led a rough, and at times a wild and dangerous life. Tall, craggy-faced, forbidding looking, he spoke in a loud, gravely harsh voice; and when he issued an order it had to be obeyed without delay. His children later described him as the epitome of the "rugged individualist." By contrast Leah, an intelligent and spirited young woman, radiated gentleness, warmth and affection and understanding.

It was even more curious that the religious, erudite, almost saintly Abbe accepted as a son-in-law this rough diamond of a young man, who for years had not set foot in a synagogue, let alone said his daily prayers according to Jewish tradition. He was not only a non-observant, non-religious Jew, he could hardly be called a Jew at all!

However father and daughter detected in Theodore something that less discerning observers had failed to see, namely a man of integrity, honest and upright, with a strong, sterling character.

Sojourn in Rockdale Texas and Return to New York

Shortly after the wedding, Theodore decided to rejoin his brother Marcus Crohn and Israel Baum, who were operating a dry goods store in Rockdale, Texas, a town so small that it did not appear on any map, and took his new bride with him. There, exactly nine months later, Leah gave birth to her first child, Esther. As his son Lawrence observed, "Papa was not one to delay doing what came naturally."

A magazine article described what the town of Rockdale must have been like in 1882:

"Rockdale with a population of 2,000 was a town where, on Saturday afternoon, farmers from all around would drive into town with their families in wagons hitched up to a team of horses. Mama and the girls,. scrubbed and in their stiff-starched Saturday's best, sat in cane-bottomed chairs. In the back were baskets of eggs, a half-dozen or so chickens with their feet tied together, and the weeks' accumulation of surplus butter. Every house within the small business district had signposts along the curb which said: 'Five dollars fine if you hitch here!' Since cattle roamed around at large, one of them might get her front feet up in the back of the wagon and eat most of a sack of flour and strew the rest of it over the street. In the middle of the afternoon, after the men had their fill of drink, the brawling started. People got drunk, and hollered and fought each other on the main street with knives, brass knuckles, billiard cues, and white-hickory axe handles. In those days, if the weevils or the droughts or the floods destroyed the cotton, we as a community were destitute."

In addition to selling dry goods and other merchandise, the three merchant brothers financed cotton planting farmers for most of the year, and when the crops finally came in, the farmers paid their bills. It was a difficult, risky livelihood at best, and life in the small town was dull and monotonous. Leah was sad and lonely, missed her friends and family in New York, and eventually persuaded her husband to give up the store, sell out and return north. Theodore received $25,000 for his interest in the form of twenty-five one thousand dollar bills, which he sewed into the lining of his shoes. On the train north he was inveigled into a poker game with strangers.

> "How did you make out?" his sons once asked him.
> "Well, from Texarkana to St. Louis I lost three thousand dollars."
> "What?" they cried.
> "Yes, but between St. Louis and New York I won back the three thousand and two thousand dollars more."

In New York two things occurred. He became a member of the fledgling Consolidated Stock Exchange, and for the rest of his life made a living in Wall Street, at times precariously, selling shares of stock in odd lots, and trading for his own account. The other event was that he came under the influence of his father-in-law Abbe Baum, and became a fervent, ultra-zealous convert to strict orthodox Judaism; and for the rest of his life was intensely, almost fanatically, religious. As his oldest son Burrill put it,

> "He said his prayers in Hebrew night and day, at home and in the synagogue, before meals and after meals, all day Saturday and on all the numerous holy days, and never understood one word of what he was reciting."

Theodore tried for years, without success, to coerce his sons to follow his example; but his wife Leah, who inherited her father Abbe Baum's more spiritual and esthetic approach to religion, was a far greater influence on their children.

A Family of Twelve Children

The family moved from one house to another in the early years, first to a wooden house on East 86th Street, followed by one at 216 East 82nd Street, and finally to the large five-story brownstone at 70 East 92nd Street, where most of their twelve children grew up.

When the famous blizzard of 1888 struck, the family was still living in the two-story wooden house on East 86th Street. "That day," Theodore's daughter Esther, then six years old later recalled, "I walked downstairs to the street floor to find the rooms freezing cold and in total darkness. The entire house was completely snowed in. But a family of hungry children needed food. So Papa had to shovel a path from the rooftop to the sidewalk so that he could slide down and go to buy provisions. There were no refrigerators or freezers in those days."

Leah, it seems, was always pregnant. She was nursing one infant while at the same time carrying another. All the children were delivered at home in their mother's huge, old-fashioned oak-carved bed. Delivery was easy, her son Burrill recalled. "She just plopped them out without complications." All that was needed was an old-fashioned home nurse and a quick messenger to summon Dr. Samuel J. Meltzer when the time arrived. "Incidentally," Burrill added, "it is interesting to remember how one sent for the doctor in those days. There was no telephone of course. Dr. Meltzer's office was at 112th Street and Madison Avenue. I was given carfare and took the Madison Avenue horse-car to his office. Sometime later the doctor would arrive in his horse-drawn carriage," and not always on time.

Leah and Theodore Crohn

Leah wanted desperately to limit her endless pregnancies but her husband refused. He believed literally in the biblical injunction, "Be fruitful and multiply!" "When I became a medical student and later on an intern," Burrill wrote, "my mother would beg me to help her have an abortion. But my father wouldn't permit her even to use a vaginal douche after intercourse. In her late pregnancies, she would jump, fall and do anything violently physical to bring on an abortion, but with her nothing availed."

New York City in the 1880s

All the streets were cobble-stoned. Telegraph poles and wires lined the sidewalks. Brewery and ice wagons were pulled by powerful horses. There were no automobiles. The well-to-do had their carriages and the rest traveled by horse-car. The center of the city's commercial and residential life was still below 59th Street. Many of the streets of what is now the upper East Side had not even been laid out. There were cow pastures and squatters farms along the park on upper Fifth Avenue, and sheep and goats occasionally roamed along Madison Avenue. What is now the Bronx was largely farm country.

"A loaf of bread," Burrill recalled, "cost five cents, and I usually received a cookie from the grocer for being such a good customer. On holidays my father would send me to the corner saloon to fill a huge silver tankard with beer, which cost ten cents. When, on occasion we ran out of milk, my mother would send me to a farm on

Sutton Place South near the East River to get an additional supply."

The House on East 92nd Street

It was here that most of the Crohn children–Esther, Burrill, Gurtha, Myron, Josh, Lawrence, Naomi, David, George, Marcella and Rosalie grew up. A twelfth child, Ada, died in infancy.

According to a family chronicle written by Lawrence Crohn, there were five stories. The basement was entered through an iron gate. You pulled the old-fashioned chain bell to gain entrance. In the front was the family dining room with a huge table and thirteen chairs around it. A hall connected the dining room with the kitchen, which contained a large coal- and wood-burning stove, an ice box, and three washtubs. Behind the kitchen was a small back yard where the laundry was hung and the children played games. "There was an outhouse too, very necessary since there was only one toilet on the third floor and one on the fourth, serving the needs of eleven children, two parents, three in help–sixteen in all."

The second floor was the formal part of the house. The long front parlor was furnished in Victorian style with large oil paintings on satin damask walls, an antique gilt curio cabinet filled with ivories, jeweled snuff boxes and other objets d'art, which Leah picked up in antique shops, and a large Steinway piano. This was the formal room where "swell" company was entertained and where suitors and future husbands called and courted the various Crohn daughters. In the rear was the large dining room, with its massive carved-oak furniture upholstered in rich blue velvet, which Leah picked up at an auction. A dumbwaiter, traveling up and down to the kitchen was operated by hand rope to bring up meals on special occasions such as Rosh Hashonah and Passover, or when special guests were entertained. The family's finest silver, china and linens were reserved for these state occasions.

On the third floor was the parents' bedroom, with a huge, old-fashioned bed behind which were hung old paintings of Theodore's grandparents. In the rear was the library, containing the plays of Shakespeare, the *Arabian Nights*, and sets of the works of Dickens, George Eliot, Washington Irving, Charles Reade and the Encyclopedia–most of which were purchased from a bookseller on the installment plan for 25 cents a week.

"In this library," Lawrence Crohn noted, "Papa kept his big roll-top desk, in one drawer of which he kept locked up a supply of macaroons and of Mirror's hard candy, which I can taste to this day. We kids discovered that by removing the drawer above and putting our hands down into the locked drawer, we could extract the goodies. Papa was always mystified at their disappearance and attributed it to mice which might have gotten in through the back of the drawer. When he questioned us, we all had innocent, deadpan faces."

The fourth and fifth floors contained bedrooms, with two double beds side by side in each room, four children to each bedroom. When there were overnight guests, which there frequently were, they slept in the cracks between the beds.

Parental Influence

At meal times, Theodore summoned the family in his loud, bellowing voice, and the children would come jumping down the stairs or sliding down the banister. With fourteen or more people around the large table, Leah would sit at the head and would dole out the food, serving her husband first, filling each plate in turn and serving herself last. The Crohns had hearty appetites. His eldest son Burrill, who went on to become a world-famous physician, attributed his having chosen internal medicine as his specialty to the fact that his father had always suffered from indigestion and constipation.

"My father," he recalled, "went upstairs to sleep on Saturday afternoons after a very heavy dinner. One Saturday afternoon I heard someone stomping about and falling upstairs. I went up to find my father stumbling around, evidently drunk. I looked and saw the enema bag he had been using hanging from the bedpost. The bag still contained the remains of witch hazel which contains a large percentage of alcohol, with which it had been filled. He was drunk on rectally-absorbed witch hazel!"

Theodore was a stern father, abrupt, impatient, irascible, and easily irritated. Yet he impressed strangers and could be kind, courtly and gracious, especially towards the ladies for whom he had quite an "eye"; and his reputation for integrity and good character in the community and on Wall Street was of the highest. He believed in and lived by his principles.

But it was Leah who was the rock and foundation on which the Crohn family life depended. She was, as her son Burrill described her, "a mother of exceptional maternal instinct, a womanly spirit to her family and friends, a rock of support to her children, and so amiable and lovable a character, so benevolent, easy going and kindly disposed, never ruffled, that she summed up in her personality all that could be crowded into the blessed word 'mother.'"

A sensitive, articulate writer, Burrill's picture of his mother may sound overly sentimental. Still his words seem to ring true.

The children looked forward to being sick so that they could share the huge, old-fashioned bed with her. "I can still remember," Burrill wrote, "being rocked in her arms to sleep as a sick child, still hear her mellow, beautiful soprano voice singing me to sleep, still feel the warmth of her full round arms, her olive skin, her soft kindly hands and her sudden impulsive kisses for the cute babies of which she never tired."

Feeding and Clothing a Large Family

Leah was an expert manager. Theodore gave her twenty-five dollars a week for food and help and other sundry expenses. On this she had to run a household of sixteen. Although this allowance wasn't much money, so many families in those days were living in abject poverty that the Crohns considered themselves comparatively well off, and enjoyed life, although they grew up without the benefit of movies, radio or television.

On Monday morning, Leah would take out her big pocketbook and dole out pocket money, five cents a week for the oldest child, three cents for the next, two cents for the others and a penny for the babies.

"In the afternoon," Burrill wrote, "she would dress the children as they came in from the back yard, dirty but happy, their faces smeared with a spoonful of dough or the molasses cake which Becky, the cook, was baking, stolen from the kitchen when her back was turned. Dressed in her old half negligee wrapper over her perspiring figure, washing this child's face, combing another's hair in spite of tears and struggles, directing one to change his shoes, another to put on fresh pants, sending one to the grocer, another to the bakery–all done in feverish haste. No child talked back to her, no one disobeyed; for kindly and loving as she was, the magnitude of her tasks demanded obedience from all. And she never failed to elicit it."

The necessity of providing innumerable articles of clothing for such a large family forced Leah to search for ways of shopping in the most economical way. She haunted the stores downtown on 23rd Street, 34th Street and elsewhere–Hearn's, O'Neill's, Stern Bros., Altmans, Gammeyer, Siegel-Cooper, and Wannamaker–searching for bargains. When the bills came in after the first of the month, she would hide them and dole them out to Theodore one at a time, taking the scolding as he shouted at her with each one, saving the biggest for last, promising not to buy anything more, and starting all over again a few days later at her same old shopping haunts downtown.

"Mother's shopping bills," recalled her son Lawrence, "were especially heavy twice each year, once for the High Holidays and once for Passover, when we were all newly outfitted. She bought assorted sizes for the boys and girls in dozen lots. How often our bell would ring and Nora, our maid, would throw the packages from the various department stores into the ash-can closet and shut the door, to hide them from Papa, who was reading Psalms in the front dining room. We were six husky boys. Pants always wore out or grew too tight sooner than the jackets. So mother would take us to Uncle Eddie Epstein's factory to replenish trousers. If they didn't match the surviving jackets, it was just too bad. Yet Papa never ceased to go into tirades over the bills. Mother never seemed unduly perturbed. But she did finally have a nervous breakdown, perhaps as the result of bearing twelve children and experiencing the tensions of a huge household without tranquilizers on hand. But she soon recovered, and was her normal self again."

Burrill recalled anxiously waiting for her to come home from one of those shopping jaunts downtown. Six o'clock, six-thirty, dinner time, Theodore furious. "At seven I sneaked out, and knowing her habits ran around to Third Avenue and 83rd Street and watched each El train coming uptown to see if she would descend from the platform to the street. The dusk grew deeper. I cried, I knew some dreadful accident had happened to Mama–and still she did not come. Finally, around 7:30, I saw her swaying down the avenue, arms full of bundles, tired, unafraid of the inevitable scolding surely in store for her, but elated with her wonderful day of shopping."

Household Help

Of course a family of that size had help. In those days women went way downtown to Castle Garden to select household help from immigrants arriving from Europe. The Crohns had Becky Adler, a young woman from Austria, as cook. In addition to cooking all the family meals, Becky made magnificent pastries, coffee cake, molasses cake, ruglach (small crescent-shaped cakes filled with nuts and sugar), and large home-baked challahs, the Sabbath loaves, all baked in the iron coal and wood stove. Extra challahs were made for relatives and older members of the family who had married, which the younger children took turns in delivering. "Sometimes we got a nickel tip," recalled Lawrence Crohn.

In addition, Leah brought home two young Irish women, Agnes Dunn and later Nora Kelleher, who served as "upstairs girls." Once a week a visiting laundress came to the house to wash and iron for the entire family. The washing was done in the two huge tubs adjoining the kitchen. The heavy pressing irons had to be heated on the kitchen stove. There were no laundromats, washing machines or driers in those days; nor dishwashers, electric ice-boxes or freezers. The iceman came every day.

In spite of the hard work that the girls performed each day, Agnes and Nora loved Leah, and though they left briefly to marry, they later returned. Becky Adler remained with the family for forty-three years. "The benignity of Leah's character and personality, and her own tireless activity," he son Burrill wrote, "was the lodestar that held them in spite of the mass of work that was crowded into each day, and converted ordinary working girls into admiring slaves."

Illness, Worry and Tragedy

Every year the various children, as they grew up, went through the gamut of children's diseases and domestic epidemics–scarlet fever, measles, dyptheria, whooping cough and the rest. As each infant became ill he or she was carried to their mother's big bed in the front room, to lie there feverishly, studying the picture of the reindeer and the little fawn on the opposite wall, and to sleep with Mama at night in the same bed. "It was," as Burrill put it, "a privilege to be sick, an actual pleasure to be nursed by her and by her alone, her loving touch, the cool sponge, her affectionate embrace. It was hard to discover whether she loved the girls better or took pride more in the boys. They were the softer dew of her older age, the little characters that were going to resemble her and grow each into an image, a resemblance of her own soul, character and endeavor."

If it was scarlet fever, the other children were rushed off to the houses of one of their aunts until the contagious period was over.

Her crowded life provided Leah with endless problems, but she never seemed to worry, never was anxious about possible evils befalling the children. For several summers the family spent its vacation at a small farm house in the Catskill Mountains. At the end of one such vacation, one hot night early in September, Leah entrusted her oldest boy, Burrill, to take a part of her unwieldy family, six children, one a baby, and two maids, on the Hudson River night boat from the Catskills down to New York. She had tried to reserve staterooms but it was the Labor Day weekend, the boat was overcrowded and only one small berth was available. Becky and the baby were in the berth, and the rest of them slept on the floor. Some years later, Burrill asked his mother if she had been concerned or anxious at the time. "No," she replied, "I knew nothing would happen." She was by nature an optimist, never suspected malice in others and never expected evil to fall upon her children, and fortunately it never did.

However, the loss of her little girl, Ada, was a tragedy with which she could never reconcile herself. One day little Ada, eight years old, was playing on the beach at Long Branch in New Jersey, a happy, healthy child. But that night she suddenly came down with a sudden high fever that none of the doctors who were summoned could comprehend, and the next morning she was dead. Some years later, Leah having returned to the city in the fall, was cleaning the house which had been closed for the summer. She was in the basement arranging the clothes when she suddenly came upon one little shoe of the little girl who had been taken so suddenly away from her. Her boy Burrill happened to witness the incident. "Her sobs, her unrestrained crying, the kisses she poured over that shoe," Burrill noted, "were so clearly and sadly impressed on my childish memory, that from that day to this, that little tearful incident has always stood out as the symbol of her overpowering love for all her children, and as the token of love of all mothers for all children."

For Leah, the World War was another fearful ordeal. Four of the Crohn sons enlisted in the Army or Navy and served overseas. Recalling the suffering of his mother during this period, Burrill wrote:

> "As she sat with her failing eyesight poring over the daily list of casualties, afraid, yet looking under the names beginning with 'C' for the frightful catastrophes that might come, she made a pitiable but brave figure, confident in the right and convinced with an undying faith that no harm would come to her boys."

Only when Armistice Day finally arrived was she finally relieved of that daily pain.

Mother and Grandmother – A Never Ending Devotion

As the children one by one grew up, during the years of adolescence, courtship and marriage, while Theodore was the strict respected disciplinarian, Leah remained for each of them their confidante, the rock of advice; and when in later years they returned on so many occasions to visit their parents' home, they always found her an interested listener.

"Whether in her own home," Burrill wrote, "or in our more recently established homes, she was always there when you needed her, with her package of home-made cakes under her arm, a book for the grandchildren, or a box of candy, an old photograph of a son as a baby newly rediscovered to be handed with pride to her daughter-in-law; in the rain, in the oppressive heat of a

July day, her tired, heavy form could be seen mounting the stairs, an unexpected but always welcome guest."

"Even in the terrible flu epidemic of 1918, when we in our 81st Street house were all sick, when every maid had deserted, when no one dared to visit such a house, who walks in one day slowly climbing the stairs, with a big bowl of fish and gravy still warm from her own stove, but Mama. Afraid? Not she! Scoldings didn't help; she went as she willed–streetcars, long steep stairs, the heat of August, the bitter cold of March, all one to her so long as she could help–a ray of sunshine to lighten our depression."

"As for her husband Theodore, her lifelong steady companion, her affection never ended, failed or weakened. Loyalty, devotion and service to him, him above all, that came first. No greater diplomat ever lived, no one more tactful and judicious in every situation, yielding before the storm and coming back more resilient than ever. No more womanly woman, and, referring to Leah's biblical namesake, no more affectionate Leah serving her Jacob than this one! During their forty-one years together she never questioned his authority or disobeyed his commands. He was the master of the household and his word was law. At the same time, she never lost her sweet and affectionate disposition."

A Religious Household

Needless to say, the Sabbath and the numerous Jewish holy days were strictly observed in the Crohn household. Sabbath services started Friday night and continued on Saturday afternoon, with afternoon and evening services following the midday meal. Most holiday services, as well, started the evening before with most of the following day devoted to prayers. Everyone attended the old synagogue on East 82nd Street in those days. In any case, there was nothing else to do.

Weekdays, they were required to get up early enough to say their prayers before breakfast. "We boys," Burrill recalled, "would line up with our prayer books in front of us, but the conversation was about whether the Giants and the Dodgers baseball teams had won their games the day before. There was no radio or TV then, and we had to wait for the early morning paper for the sports results. Suddenly the shadow of the Old Man was spied coming downstairs to the basement, and we would begin reciting our prayers at the top of our voices. Papa would enter the room and say 'Good boys! Good Boys' and we would quickly have breakfast and rush off to school."

On weekdays, after public school, the Crohn boys had to attend Hebrew school in the basement of the synagogue, which was dark and dingy with only a single gaslight. They were bored with the recitations of the texts and translations from the Bible and learned little.

"My father," Burrill wrote, "went to synagogue dressed in tails and a high silk hat, a 'stove-pipe' we called it, all silk and polished. If it rained, I had to accompany him, holding an open umbrella over his high hat. As he was tall and I was small, this entailed considerable effort on my part to keep that umbrella over that precious hat. He couldn't carry the umbrella himself because that would be 'work,' disallowed on the Sabbath according to strict orthodox injunctions. He wasn't even allowed to 'carry' a handkerchief, which was therefore tied around his waist."

"Since I was carrying the umbrella, wasn't I committing a sin, I asked. 'Yes, but you are not yet Bar Mitzvah (thirteen),' he explained. 'Until that day your sins do not count!'"

One Friday evening, on the way to synagogue, walking with his father, Burrill saw a penny on the sidewalk. Since carrying money on the Sabbath was forbidden, he dared not pick it up. What to do? Carefully he kicked the penny into a crack in the pavement and covered it with dirt. On Saturday evening, on the way home, he carefully retrieved his penny.

During the so-called High Holidays and the ten Penitential Days, Theodore would wake his sons up at dawn to accompany him to synagogue each day. Of course there was no time for breakfast, which was a hardship, especially on the late fall days when the synagogue in the early morning was cold. One day, Burrill recalled, they were all ready to depart when they were joined by his brother Josh at the front stoop. "Good boys!" said Theodore. Little did he know that Josh, who had been out all night on a date, was dressed in his evening clothes under his overcoat, which he dared not remove for the rest of the day.

During synagogue services, Theodore had little patience for long-winded rabbinical sermons, and as an important member of the congregation and later its president, he did not hesitate to let his views be known.

"The rabbi, Rabbi Peikes," Burrill wrote, "worked as a paper box salesman on weekdays, which was not unusual at that time when rabbinical salaries were very modest. His English was imperfect and he wrote out his sermons in a large script so that he could hide the text and appear to be speaking extemporaneously. It was my job to read over the text during the preliminary prayers and correct the mistakes." When he spoke too long, Theodore grew hungry, having had no breakfast, and would bang loudly on his prayer book, growl, "Enough already" and bring the sermon to an end.

The McKinley Incident and A Missed Investment Opportunity

Although the stock exchange was open on Saturdays and Jewish holidays, Theodore Crohn was in synagogue and the transaction of any business on such days was of course unthinkable. In an emergency, his Christian friend George Turton would look out for Theodore's interests downtown. One Friday night in 1901, as the family left the old synagogue they heard the newsboys shouting "Extra! Extra! President McKinley Shot!"

His father, Burrill recalled, turned pale. Just that morning he had bought thousands of shares of stock on margin, expecting the market to go up. Now it was inevitable that the market would plummet and he would be wiped out. Burrill insisted that his father go downtown the first thing in the morning to take care of matters, but he refused. "Never on the Sabbath!" he said. Burrill went over to see Rabbi Peikes, who advised that a special dispensation from strict religious regulations might be granted, according to the Talmud, in case of dire emergencies; but Theodore would have none of it. He didn't eat any supper, and walked the floor all night unable to sleep. At eight o'clock he woke up Burrill and told him to call his friend George Turton at quarter to ten, just before the market opened (Theodore himself wouldn't use the telephone on the Sabbath), and tell him "to sell me out regardless"; and with that we went off to synagogue.

The market on Saturday opened in a panic, with shares dropping precipitously. George Turton, however, wisely didn't sell immediately, holding off until a false report came over the wire that McKinley was not seriously wounded, and when the market rebounded upward, Turton sold Theodore's shares at what proved to be a minor loss. Of course the news of McKinley's recovery was premature. They did not know of the bullet lodged in his pancreas, and a few days later the President died.

True to the Baum-Webster-Crohn family tradition, Theodore late in life almost made a fortune in real estate–almost but not quite. Characteristically, his religious convictions stood in the way.

He decided, like some of his wealthy friends at the synagogue, to invest in "property" and poured his entire life savings in the purchase of an apartment house on Park Avenue near 90th Street, a neighborhood that was starting to become fashionable. Unfortunately, Theodore being occupied downtown all week, his superintendent would wait until Saturday to confront Theodore with his manifold problems–a bursting water pipe, repairs to the furnace, tenant complaints and so forth. But Theodore refused to be bothered, telling him "Do the best you can. This is my Sabbath, I can't be disturbed!" However, the problems mounted and were often too much for his super, with the result that Theodore decided abruptly to sell the property, losing an investment that a few years later became immensely valuable.

Music played an important role in the Crohn family home. Leah communicated her love of good music to all the children, and her natural talent and beautiful though untrained soprano voice enabled her to cultivate friendships with gifted musicians like her next-door neighbor Mr. Velton, an eminent concert violist, who would come to the house to perform at musicales in the back parlor before specially invited audiences. Then Leah would be accompanied as, in her ringing clear soprano, she would sing "Stille wie die Nacht," "Jerusalem" and "The Messiah."

"How we used to thrill at her full vocal melodies," recalled Burrill, "as we children sat in our nightgowns at the top of the stairs in the shadows as she sang, ready to scamper away at a moment's notice, lest we be surprised and observed in our surreptitious pleasure."

All the children, as they grew older, became opera buffs. When they couldn't afford to buy tickets at the old Manhattan Opera House, they enlisted as "supers" in the cast and received $1 per performance. When the new magnificent Metropolitan Opera House opened at Broadway and 39th Street, their parents became regular subscribers.

Lawrence Crohn recalled his father and mother as they departed for a performance: "Papa in his long full-dress suit, starched shirt and folding opera hat, and Mama wearing velvet befurred garments which she bought at Bendel's or other fashionable shops, or had them custom-made by a fine dressmaker. She wore a beautiful diamond 'sunburst' brooch which Papa gave her and which unfortunately she had to sell in a leaner year to help the sagging family budget. If a horse and carriage were not available, or too expensive, they ventured out in wintry weather to the Third Avenue streetcar downtown, then by the 42nd Street crosstown horse-car to the opera house, and trudged back by the same route. Later they would describe the wonderful singing of Melba, Marcella Sembrich, Mme. Schumann Heink, Alma Gluck and other famous stars. These were the days before Caruso and Martinelli."

Frequently on Saturday night there were informal family get-togethers at the Crohn house, or at the home of their cousins the Websters, who lived only a few blocks away. Those were gay evenings, with games, dancing, singing of songs around the piano, or listening to "classical" music on the family's new victrola.

It was one such night that I, a shy young boy of nine, met the Crohn family for the first time, an event I would never forget. My father and mother, Cecil and Sophie Ruskay who lived in Lawrence, Long Island, made a point of having their children occasionally visit over weekends in New York City with a cousin, so that we would have the opportunity to meet my father's various relatives–the Crohns, Baums, Websters and the rest.

On this particular weekend, on Saturday night, I was taken to the Crohn house where a family party was in progress. They were all there–the whole family–not only the still unmarried sons and daughters, but those already married with their wives or husbands. I was taken by the hand and led to the far end of the large room, where Theodore and Leah sat alongside one another, presiding over the festivities. Theodore patted me on the head, and Leah gave me a big kiss and announced: "This is Sophie's boy!" And everyone smiled and made a great fuss over me, their little country cousin. My mother Sophie, although the daughter of a well-to-do shirt manufacturing family, the Liebowitzes, with whom the far from affluent Crohns had little in common, was, due to her warm and colorful personality, very popular with my father's relatives.

Crohn Family Summers

New York City was uncomfortably hot and humid during the summer months. There was no air-conditioning of course in those days. Families that could afford to do so, departed for "the country" for the summer months–to the Catskills, the Jersey shore, the Rockaways on Long Island and elsewhere. Each year, Leah would scan the advertisements in the newspapers offering homes for summer rental, always waiting till the end of June, when houses not yet rented would be available at bargain prices. At various times, the Crohn family rented cottages in Tuckahoe and Mount Kisco in New York, in Point Pleasant, New Jersey, and in Tannersville in the Catskill Mountains. The owners who rented their homes were always astonished when their summer tenants descended on them–two parents, a cook and a tribe of as many as eleven children.

Getting to Tannersville was an expedition in itself, involving as it did a ferry ride across New York harbor to New Jersey, a long train journey on the Delaware-Lackawanna West Shore Railroad to the mountains, and a horse and buggy ride from the station to the old farm at the top of the hill. There was no electricity, just kerosene lamps and a wood-burning stove. Papa Theodore came up for the weekend each Friday afternoon. At Tannersville the family ate only breakfast at the house. Lunch and dinner were eaten at the old Fairmont Hotel, where many prominent figures in the Jewish religious community and in the Zionist movement were frequent guests. Many years later, I and a friend together with my father Cecil Ruskay, in the course of a week's hiking in that part of the Catskills, descended at noon one hot day early in September, into Tannersville, sweaty, tired and hungry, and entered the Fairmont Hotel dining room. The proprietress, the granddaughter of the Jacobson family who had owned the hotel for over fifty years, came over and introduced herself, and, on hearing that Cecil was a close relative of the Crohn family, entertained us with stories of the Crohn children whom she remembered as frequent guests when she was a child.

Later on, the Crohns spent their summers at the Rockaway shore, first in Hammels and thereafter at a house purchased by Theodore in Arverne, two blocks from the ocean. Arverne was at that time the fashionable summer resort for many middle- and upper-class New York Jewish families. The Liebowitz, Unterberg, Pels, and other well-to-do Jewish families occupied mansions near the ocean. It was here that Burrill Crohn met his first wife, the beautiful Lucile Pels, and his cousin Cecil Ruskay, whose family then in straitened circumstances spent the summer in a tent

Top Row: Theodore Crohn, Ben Shapiro, Laurie Crohn
Middle Row: Esther, Dan, Gurtha, Myron and Leah Crohn
Bottom Row: Naomi Crohn, Grandma Goldie Baum, Marcella
             and Rosalie Crohn

colony on the nearby Edgemere beach, met his future wife, Sophie Liebowitz.

A veritable gang of people benefited from the Crohn summer house in Averne. Aunts and cousins spent weeks at a time there. In addition, each child was permitted to invite a special friend for one weekend during the season. When the older Crohn daughters married and had children, they rented rooms across the street, but only for the purpose of sleeping. They had all their meals at the house. Relatives didn't bother to notify the family in advance. On Sunday they just calmly trooped in. Poor Becky, the cook, just piled on more food, and the Crohn boys were sent to the ice house to get additional huge cakes of ice for the crude wood ice-cream freezer, which made home-made ice-cream.

Upstairs, a room was reserved for Grandma Goldie, Leah's mother, the widow of Abbe Baum, who spent her summers there. "I remember," recalled Lawrence Crohn, "looking into her trunks and seeing there quantities of loose candy scattered among her clothes, and, of all things, her burial shroud."

It was here too, that Doctor Burrill Crohn, finished with his internship, started the practice of medicine. In his "office," a sitting room downstairs, Aunt Millie Baum, who complained of a sore throat, was told by Burrill to gargle with a yellow mixture she would find there, only to discover later that the "mixture" was really a urine specimen.

Celebrating the Jewish Holidays

The Friday night meal that commenced the Sabbath was a festive occasion in the Crohn household. Lawrence Crohn recalled:

> "Before the meal began Theodore would bless each child individually, asking the Almighty to have them follow in the footsteps of heroic male and female figures of the old Testament. Starting with the oldest, Esther, he placed his hands on her head and recited the words: 'May God make you like Sarah, Rebecca, Leah and Rachel.' Then, beginning with Burrill, he would intone: 'May God make you like Ephraim and Manasah.' Each of us stood in line in order of our age. It was a chore for us since we had to kiss Papa after the blessing, and his whiskers tickled us. But we were always respectful. Woe betide us if we weren't."
>
> "Then Leah started serving the food. Everything at the table was lined up with tureens and platters in front of her–gefilte fish, chicken soup and other dishes served in huge portions to her family. She just managed to take a few mouthfuls for herself before we were demanding second helpings. There were never less than three oversize pies for dessert."

After the meal there was the family "benching," the grace after meals with its traditional melodies that Grandpa Abbe Baum had taught, including the last verse of the final prayer, which was sung to the tune of "America" ("My Country t'is of Thee"). The result was quite a chorus, Leah with her lyric soprano, Naomi's contralto voice, Lawrence the baritone, Myron the basso profundo and Marcella with her childish, melodious treble. It must have sounded impressive because passers-by in the street would stop in front to listen to the

Crohn chorus and remain standing there to the conclusion.

After the Friday night supper, Theodore took out the Bible and read the portion of the week in English. Then the whole family strolled down Madison Avenue and Theodore would hold forth on the rapid expansion of the city. At bed time, the gas jets had to be turned off, another operation that was forbidden to be performed by religious Jews. If Nora, the Irish maid, was out, a gentile neighbor had to be found to do this. Once a big, burly Irishman came in. After turning off the jets he turned to the six stropping Crohn sons and growled, "What the hell is wrong with you guys? Couldn't you blow them out?"

On Saturday mornings Theodore left for synagogue at 7:30 A.M. His sons left later but were supposed to be in their seats at 9:30. The Crohns had their own family pew, with Theodore always occupying the aisle seat. As they arrived, his sons had to slip past their father, and would receive a vigorous kick in the shins if they were late.

In the fall, the High Holidays started. First came the ten Penitential Days when Theodore would wake up his sons at 4:00 A.M. to accompany him to synagogue in the early dawn. Then came the two day celebration of Rosh Hashannah, the Jewish New Year. On the afternoon of the first day Theodore and a group of his friends went to the Central Park reservoir to perform an ancient rite–the symbolic casting of their sins into the sea. "A few Psalms were recited," the family chronicle relates, "and the words of the Prophet Micah were intoned. They threw a few pebbles or twigs into the water, symbolizing the remission of their sins."

Shortly before Yom Kippur, the Day of Atonement, another strange, ancient ritual dating from the middle ages was performed. "A few live chickens were brought into our cellar. Papa waved a screeching chicken over the head of each child, and intoned a prayer. Supposedly the animal was expected to assume our sins, which were transferred to it. The next morning, a little bearded man came and slit the throats of the doomed chickens." Later on, this ritual of animal sacrifice as an atonement for sins was disapproved of and discontinued.

When the full moon started each month, Theodore took each of his sons to the back yard, where each one was blessed and, in turn, wished one another good health and prosperity for the coming month.

During the Succoth holidays, the Feast of Tabernacles, an outdoor tent with a lattice-like roof was constructed in the back yard and decorated with fruits and vegetables and paper chains hung on evergreen branches. There, for the week, the entire family managed to take its meals squeezed into the little booth, commemorating the lifestyle of the children of Israel as they wandered through the wilderness of Sinai, on the way to the Promised Land.

Chanukhah, around Christmas time, and Purim were enjoyable holidays. On Purim, after synagogue there was a family masquerade party at the home of their cousins the Websters. Everyone had to come in a costume. The men dressed up as women, in corsets and camisoles, and danced and sang as chorus girls. The gaiety went on until the wee hours of the morning.

The Passover festival came in the Spring. For days the house had to be cleaned from top to bottom to be sure that all leavened bread, cake and candy, including even small quantities of bread or cake crumbs, were removed from the cupboards and closets. "The night before the Seder," Lawrence Crohn wrote, "Papa went into each room with a box and a chicken feather to gather up little crumbs which his son Burrill had hidden in advance"–a ceremony intended to symbolize the complete removal of all leavened bread and food from the house.

On Seder night, there was always a new youngster to ask the Four Questions. Theodore read the Haggadah, the story of the slavery of the Jews in Egypt and their escape across the Red Sea "with serious concentration," Lawrence went on, " while *we* were concentrating on the wonderful food ahead!"–soup, hard-boiled eggs in salt water, gefilte fish, roast and the ritualistic glasses of wine for each person that made everyone a bit giddy.

Shortly thereafter came the Fast of Tisha B'av, commemorating the fall of Jerusalem and the dispersal and exile of the Jews to Arabic countries. This was a holiday the family would never forget, "for it was on the eve of Tisha B'av" wrote Lawrence Crohn, "that our mother Leah suffered her last agony," dying that evening at Mount Sinai hospital from peritonitis, resulting from a burst appendix, at the age of 64. At the time antibiotics and penicillin, which would have saved her life, had not yet been discovered. The entire family, her children, her brothers and sisters, surrounded her bedside. Her son Burrill, already an established physician, recalled "I gave her her last morphine injections so she would not linger helplessly in pain."

Then everyone recited the Shma Yisroel as she closed her eyes for the last time.

Doctor Henry Morais, the dour, outspoken son of the founder of the Jewish Theological Seminary, delivered the eulogy at the funeral service. Pointing to the Crohn children, he asserted that they were not worthy of such a mother. Leah would have disagreed.

Theodore's Final Days

After his wife's death, Theodore kept up the family home for a while with his son Burrill, then divorced, and Josh, as well as his Aunt Mallie Baum living with him. Burrill's daughter, Ruth Dickler, then a young girl who lived with them, remembered her grandfather as always immersed in his books. When Burrill took his own apartment, with all his children now married, Theodore moved in with the family of his daughter Gurtha Roth in Cedarhurst, Long Island. By this time, he had been defeated by Wall Street. Most of his living expenses were now provided by the generosity of his sons Josh and Burrill. He kept busy with his occasional involvement with his old synagogue, dropping in on the local brokerage offices and playing pinochle, at which he was an expert. But most of his time was spent poring over his Hebrew and other books.

Few, if any, of Theodore's children in later life followed their father's rigid orthodox religious way of life. Rather, like so many others, their synagogue attendance was largely confined to the High Holidays and they observed only the most important religious ceremonies in their homes. But they loved and revered their father, enjoyed in retrospect the strict regimen which they were required to follow while growing up, and became nostalgic in remembering them and describing them to their own children and grandchildren.

Theodore's death came in his eighty-sixth year, at Gurtha's home in Cedarhurst. He slumped to the floor in the upstairs bathroom and died instantly of heart failure. The door of the bathroom was locked and the water was still running. His grandson, Martin, had to borrow a high ladder from the local fire department to enable him to climb through the small bathroom window to unlock the door from the inside. The evening before, he had been playing billiards with his sons, following it with a game of pinochle. At the time of his death he was reading the *Life of Mohammed* and the *History of the Jesuit Order*. In his spare moments he made a habit of reading the encyclopedia.

His son Lawrence wrote of him: "It could be said of Theodore that he was a good American, a good Jew, a good family man, and a good Democrat."

CHAPTER III

BURRILL

Burrill, the oldest son of Theodore and Leah Crohn, was fond of saying that he was conceived in Rockdale, Texas, a town so small that it could not be found on any map, where his father owned a dry good store in partnership with his brother Marcus and his brother-in-law Israel Baum. However, he added, he was born on June 13, 1884 at 216 East 82nd Street in New York City, after his father had sold out his interest and moved North. At that time, some of the streets of the upper East Side were not yet laid out, and occasionally nanny goats and cows would wander over from pasture land along upper Fifth Avenue.

"Our family physician," Burrill recalled, "was Doctor Samuel J. Meltzer, whose office was at 122nd Street. There was no telephone, and when my mother's time for my delivery was imminent, my father ran to Madison Avenue and took the horse-car to the doctor's office. Some time later Dr. Meltzer arrived at the house in his horse-drawn carriage, but by then I was already under the bed clothes. The doctor, a big, portly man with a thick German accent, but gentle and kind and very devoted to the family, picked up the baby, slapped him on the backside and said, "Was ist dass?" Little did he know that the infant would one day succeed him as President of the American Gastroenterological Association, of which Dr. Meltzer was one of the founders.

Early Education

Burrill attended P.S. 77 at 88th Street and First Avenue, from which he was graduated at the age of thirteen. There were no high schools in those days; one went directly from public school to college. "I took the city-wide competitive examination for City College–two hundred boys with the highest marks were selected–and was admitted. The minimum age for admission was fourteen, but my father lied about my age. It was probably the only lie that my father, a man of impeccable probity, ever told.

"C.C.N.Y. was at 23rd Street and Lexington Avenue and we lived at 82nd Street, three miles away. My father gave me fifty cents a week for car fare, saying, 'If you need more pocket money, learn to walk.' I did so and have been a brisk walker ever since. I walked both ways every day, with my cousin Cecil Ruskay, who was at City College at the same time. Walking saved a nickel, which purchased two pretzels and three over-ripe bananas for lunch. On Saturday nights there was a poker game at the house of my cousins, the Websters, where I usually lost whatever car fare I had saved."

In 1902 at the age of eighteen Burrill was graduated from City College. For a while he considered going into law or business, as many of his friends did, but in the end chose medicine, and was immediately admitted to the College of Physicians and Surgeons of Columbia University.

Medical School and Internship

During his first year at medical school he helped pay his tuition, about $400 per year, by teaching English to new immigrants at night. But in the second year he was obliged to give that up. "I had to study anatomy and physiology from 10 P.M. to 1 A.M. and sometimes to 4 A.M. I had no trouble staying awake since my room at home on the top floor was always ice-cold, the heat from the furnace in the cellar never reaching there. But I began to lose the ability to concentrate on my studies because of exhaustion and lack of sleep."

His life-long interest in laboratory research began at medical school. At the suggestion of one of his professors, he and another student friends carried out a lengthy experiment on a dog, bleeding it internally in order to discover the effect of a massive internal hemorrhage on the chemistry of the body. For weeks they had to gather the food, urine and stool of the animal, dry it, crush it to powder and then analyze it for its chemical contents. As the result of this extra experimental work conducted late at night, they were awarded at graduation, in addition to their M.D. degrees, the degrees of M.A. and PhD. from Columbia.

"I accepted the extra degrees," Burrill said, "but declined the parchment certificates. I didn't have the heart to ask my father for the additional sixty dollars that they cost."

In those days third and fourth year medical students learned obstetrics by being sent downtown to the lower East Side and delivering the babies of expectant mothers. "One early experience was most difficult for me and the mother-to-be," Burrill said. "The patient, a young woman in an old tenement house, went into labor and was having a hard time, it being her first child. Labor continued all day through the first day and through the mid-August night, and all through the second day and second night. The tenement was hot, humid and airless. Being on duty, I was not supposed to sleep and, in any case, there were so many fleas, mosquitoes and cockroaches that it was impossible to lie down. Every six hours I delivered my status report back to the hospital by giving ten cents to a street urchin. Hour after hour passed with little progress and yet no special technical assistance from the hospital arrived. I was on my own."

"On the morning of the second sleepless night, exhaustion finally overcame me. Seeking some cool, fresh air about dawn, I climbed out on the outside fire escape, leaned back against the wall and fell instantly, although unwillingly, into a sound sleep, my head falling forward against my chest. A short time later I was awakened by a gentle stream of warm fluid falling on the back of my neck, and heard a woman's voice from the floor above say: 'Shame on you, you naughty boy, peeing on the good doctor!' Finally, an emergency squad arrived from the nearby Lying In Hospital with an expert surgeon, who delivered the baby safely with forceps."

Burrill and two of his classmates planned to apply for internship at Lenox Hill Hospital, then known as the German Hospital, which had an excellent department of internal medicine, which was Burrill's primary interest. Mount Sinai was the most prestigious hospital institution in the Metropolitan Area, but not knowing any of its trustees or department heads, they thought they had no chance of being accepted there. At the last minute, they decided to take the Mount Sinai exam and to their great surprise, all three were accepted.

He interned at Mount Sinai from 1907 to 1910, in pathology for one year and in internal medicine for two years. Duties on the wards were strenuous. Sleep was at a premium. Interns worked six and one-half days a week, with one night off. There were thirty-four interns to cover four hundred patients. They received no salary, only board, uniforms and laundry. No women or married men were accepted. Social intercourse between staff doctors and interns and nurses was strictly forbidden. If an intern was seen in the company of one of the nurses outside the hospital, it meant the end of the career for both of them. But such opportunities were few in any case, since there was little time off, and nurses had to be in by 10 P.M., when the gates of the hospital were locked.

At the end of his internship he received the munificent sum of fifty dollars, and a little black bag containing a stethoscope and a few other instruments essential for starting private practice.

Interns spent the morning feverishly "working up" the patient cases, particularly the new admissions. Promptly at 2 P.M., the attending physician, or surgeon strode into the ward and began his rounds, examining patients, surrounded by his entire staff. The discussions were usually on the highest scientific level, often brilliant and the intern was encouraged to offer his own viewpoint.

"One learned," Burrill said, "by listening, observing and discussion."

On Wednesday each week, interns attended the pathological conference, at which autopsy and surgical pathological material was presented and analyzed and the final evidence on the clinical case under study was presented. This was the moment when an intern learned whether or not he had been correct in his original diagnosis of the case.

The fall season was usually the most harrowing for the intern. "We were often saddled with fifteen to twenty serious cases of typhoid fever on a single night." In those days, there were no antibiotics in general use to reduce the 104-106 degree continuous body temperatures, which lasted for days. The only way to bring down the temperature was to immerse the fever-ridden patient in a portable tub of cold water, which required two porters, one or two nurses and an intern to stand by in case the patient went into shock from the sudden drop in temperature and blood pressure. This operation had to be repeated every four hours, at which time the intern was awakened, had to put on his uniform and go to the ward and stand by sleepily. Fortunately a year or two later pyramidon and aspirin came into general use, which made it possible to reduce high fevers without having to resort to the old cumbersome method.

While much of an intern's work was routine, occasionally there were exciting, even frightening incidents. One Saturday night Burrill was awakened by a harried voice on the telephone requesting him to come down to the ward immediately. Upon arriving there, he found the door closed, with all the nurses and orderlies gathered in the hall outside. Entering the ward, he saw a tall, powerfully-built man standing in the middle of the room, bellowing and shouting like a madman. The man it turned out, had been admitted a week before, hopelessly drunk and belligerent, put to sleep with a powerful hypodermic dose, and found to be seriously ill with pneumonia. Now, after a week in a hospital bed under heavy sedation and without liquor, he had suddenly regained consciousness, had developed delirium tremens and was hallucinating, brandishing a heavy glass inkwell and threatening to brain anyone who came near him. The ambulatory patients were cowering under their beds and the bed-ridden were huddled under their blankets.

"I approached him warily," Burrill recalled, "and when I was within three feet of him he shouted, 'One more step and I'll brain you!' It was 3 A.M. and though I hesitated to call the director of the hospital, I did so, nonetheless. His answer was: 'Doctor, you're in charge of the ward. It's your responsibility.'

"Meanwhile, someone had put in a call to the nearest police station and soon an elderly police officer, not much over five feet in height, arrived. I suggested that he summon additional help. 'Show him to me,' was his calm response. He entered the ward alone, walked up to the patient and said, 'Put it down,' and the man did so. 'Follow me,' said the officer, turning around and walking out the door with the patient following meekly behind him. Downstairs I took the officer aside and whispered, "How did you do it?" 'It's the blue uniform and gold buttons, especially the buttons'" he replied. 'It never fails.'"

Looking back on his internship, Burrill later observed, "Those three years of internship and laboratory work were demanding and exhausting. I got very little sleep. But that rigorous discipline of biochemistry, bacteriology and pathology, working both on the wards and in the laboratory, laid the groundwork for my later discoveries in gastroenterology.

Medical Advances and the Replacement of Primitive Methods

"It's hard to realize," Burrill observed, "how primitive our methods, how limited was our diagnostic equipment during the first decade of the century; how completely devoid we were of therapeutic drugs. There were no intravenous transfusions, no sulfonamides, no antibiotics, no aspirin. We had to rely on primitive x-rays and crude anesthesia. Research and laboratory projects that required months, or even years, at that time, later could be finished in weeks or days. The methods used were so inaccurate that every procedure had to be performed twice to insure against error."

With only crude x-rays and without precision instruments, the only way to prove or disprove a diagnosis in an obscure or unusual case was by an exploratory operation, or if the patient died, by an autopsy. But at the time it was difficult to get the consent of the family for an autopsy. Orthodox Jews wouldn't permit it. They regarded it as defiling of the body in violation of Talmudic law. Accordingly autopsies were often performed surreptitiously. Corpses were often "stolen," or a recent surgical incision from the patient's body procured by other devious means.

The transfer of blood from a blood donor to a patient was crude, costly and tedious. There was no way known how to prevent fresh blood of the donor from coagulating within minutes before it could be given to the patient. As a result, blood had to be drawn with a syringe from the donor by a tube inserted into an artery, and infused into a second tube inserted in the vein of the patient as rapidly as possible. In order to get 500 ccs of blood into a patient with a 20 cc syringe, the performance had to be repeated twenty-five times; and each time a fresh sterilized syringe had to be used. It took all morning! It was not until 1914 that an epoch making discovery was made whereby by adding a small amount of sodium citrate to the donor blood, coagulation was prevented and blood could be transferred into the patient's vein leisurely, by gravity.

Another equally valuable advance was the introduction of intravenous therapy, whereby fluids could be fed slowly into the vein of a patient from a bottle by gravity, hour after hour, now standard procedure visible in every hospital bedroom. Before that, hospitals were losing the lives of two to three children every hot night in the summer from infantile diarrhea or dehydration.

The Beginning of Private Practice and Marriage

In 1911 at the conclusion of his years of internship, Burrill went into private practice as a specialist in internal medicine. "I became interested in specializing in diseases of the stomach and intestinal tract," Burrill said,

Dr. Burrill Crohn

"because my father was a chronic sufferer from indigestion and constipation."

He started with a tiny office just large enough to allow for the examination of the occasional patient, and a couch on which he could sleep at night. He charged one to two dollars for an office visit and two to five dollars for house calls. Fortunately he was assisted in meeting his expenses during the first year by being hired as a part-time assistant to a physician with a large and lucrative general practice who needed someone with laboratory experience. His mornings were devoted to serving as an assistant, again without pay, at the biochemistry laboratory at Mount Sinai hospital; and three afternoons each week he was put in charge of its medical outpatient clinic. During the first year of practice he earned $940. In the second year his earnings rose to $1,450.

In 1912 he married Lucile Pels. He later commented, half-seriously, "I was attracted by her beauty and her playing of Beethoven's 'Appassionata Sonata' on the piano." Lucile was indeed a very lovely woman. She was also the daughter of well-to-do German-Jewish parents, who were "less than enchanted," as Burrill put it, "with a black-haired, black-mustached doctor with his little black bag, as a son-in-law." Although Lucile, a cultured woman, stimulated his interest in painting, sculpture and other graphic arts, temperamentally they were not suited to one another, and the marriage was not a happy one.

But the fault, Burrill admitted, was not entirely Lucile's. "I partially blame my constant preoccupation with medicine," he said. "My wife could never understand why I had two or three house calls to make after dinner, almost every evening; why my days were spent in the laboratory; why I had to spend every leisure moment for two years writing *Affections of the Stomach*, published in 1928; why there was no time for me to join the family for vacations."

The First World War found Burrill overwhelmed with problems. He was at the beginning of his career, not only without parents or friends to fall back on for financial help, but on the contrary, was loaded with responsibilities. His father, Theodore, now over sixty, was losing money in the stock market and called upon him regularly not only to make good his loans, but relied on him for support at home. His rich father-in-law, who was proud of his German background, not only would not assist him, he threatened Lucile and their new-born child with starvation if Burrill enlisted in the Medical Corps of the Army to fight against Germany. Four of Burrill's brothers enlisted immediately in 1917. Burrill enlisted as a volunteer in the Second Mount Sinai Medical Unit, but the war ended before the unit was sent overseas.

After the war, his private practice grew and his career at Mount Sinai flourished. In 1920 he helped form the Department of Gastroenterology at Mount Sinai, and in 1922 he was made head of the department. In 1922 he moved his private offices to 1075 Park Avenue, in a new apartment house where he had a spacious set of rooms, a small laboratory and a large x-ray machine. Some of his friends thought that this new location at 88th Street was not fashionable enough but Burrill remained there for the rest of his professional life.

However, although they soon had two fine children, Burrill and Lucile's marriage continued to deteriorate and in 1927 they agreed to an amicable divorce. They sought to avoid scandal and publicity by going to Paris for the proceedings, where Burrill established a fictitious but technically legal residence. At that time the stigma attached to a divorce was such that many of Burrill's medical associates feared that Mount Sinai would not tolerate a divorced person as head of one of its departments, but fortunately the subject was never raised.

Father and Teacher

Although his private practice and responsibilities at the hospital kept him enormously busy, Burrill nevertheless insisted on finding time for the development of his young children, in whom he was keenly interested. His daughter, Ruth Dickler, many years later vividly described what it was like to grow up with Burrill as a father.

"He was a man of enormous physical and mental energy, a man for whom there was no end to intellectual vistas, not only an expert in his field of medicine, but knowledgeable in many other things–art, history, music and literature. I can remember coming home from parties as a young girl and finding my father sitting up in bed reading. I would tell him about my evening and then he would say, 'Listen to this'; and he would read to me from Macauley's *History of England* or from Gibbon's *Decline and Fall of the Roman Empire*, selecting the lively passages that would appeal to a young girl, and so enthusiastic that it was impossible not to enjoy it with him.

"We played guessing games. Was it the Seventh or Eighth Symphony of Beethoven that he was whistling? Was it a poem of Longfellow or William Cullen Bryant that he was quoting?

"The City of New York was boundless with its opportunities and he explored them all. What didn't we see? Trinity Church, the Sub-Treasury Building where Washington took the oath of office; the tugboats docked near the Battery; the Aquarium; the Bowery and the Lower East Side. Chinatown, Little Italy, the Bronx Zoo, the Brooklyn Botanical Gardens, the Jumel Mansion, Dykeman House, the Staten Island Ferry, the Woolworth Building. You name it; we saw it.

"And where didn't we eat? In Chinese restaurants, in Sweets on the Lower East Side; in French, Russian and Japanese restaurants all over the city. Name a museum, we were there–the Museum of the American Indian and the Hispanic Museum way up on Broadway and 155th Street; the Brooklyn Museum, the Cloisters, the Metropolitan and all the others. And not everything was intellectual–there was Coney Island with hot dogs and ice-cream! I remember *Ben Hur*, and Harold Lloyd in *The Freshman*, and Al Jolson in *The Jazz Singer*. We went to the circus at the Hippodrome. And many Sunday afternoons were spent in Van Cortland Park or in Westchester open country playing baseball, hide-and-seek or cops-and-robbers.

"On special occasions he loved to flout minor rules. Every week or two Dr. A.A. Berg, the famous surgeon, used to hold medical meetings at the Harmonie Club, and a wonderful cold supper was served afterwards. It was customary for each of the doctors to take some of the delectable left-overs home with him. Father would come home after twelve, long after I was asleep. He would awaken me and sit on my bed and feed me the most wonderful, indigestible things and tell me about his day and what happened that was special. And then he's listen to what happened to me; and all the while I'd be stuffing myself with pickles and fried chicken, strudel and other goodies any mother would have had a fit about. I justified his faith and never got sick.

"He was out a great deal. Sometimes he would be gone before I woke up; but usually I would be around and sit in the bathroom and watch him shave, and he would settle my problems or make plans for my future. Sometimes he was out for dinner and the evening. Often he would be called out to see a rich patient. But somehow he always made time for me. I often went along on house calls, lugging my books or my homework, and waiting in a patient's living room or the lobby of the hospital. Sometimes he took me to medical meetings and I would listen, fascinated, and get to meet some of the most important figures in the medical world. Often I was allowed to roam the lower depths of the hospital, watching technicians in the laboratories or playing with the animals used for experiments.

"What else can I say about my father? He is brave. I learned early from him to bear physical pain gracefully, to conquer fears that had no basis in fact, to put up with discomfort, overcome problems that seemed insuperable."

Pathfinder in Medicine

From the beginning of his career, Dr. Crohn was consumed with an overwhelming interest in research. "Every moment I could spare," he later recalled, "was spent in the lab." Everywhere there were questions to be answered, clinical problems on the hospital wards which could only be solved by investigation in the biochemistry laboratories of the medical institutions. "It was my internship in pathology that sent me on the path of scientific laboratory research combined with clinical medicine." Thereafter, for the rest of his life, he pursued unorthodox paths, became a skeptic, an innovator, challenging prevailing assumptions and practices.

At the same time and by contrast, the field of internal medicine when he started his private practice in 1911, was dominated by so-called stomach specialists, most of them ambitious interlopers–mere general practitioners rather than qualified specialists. They had office hours round the clock, from 8 A.M. to 7 P.M., and were financially very successful. With many of these so-called specialists every type of stomach disorder or disturbance–indigestion, acidity, flatulence or constipation–was treated in the same way: by colonic irrigation once a week or once in ten days. Clearing out the intestinal tract by colonic irrigation was fashionable, almost a fad.

With others, everything the doctor couldn't explain, the abdominal pain of every neurotic, every nervous woman or hysterical girl with a belly ache, was called "chronic appendicitis," and the removal of the appendix was the favorite, almost routine treatment.

An incident early in his career impressed Burrill with the vital importance of clinical examinations. One day, while he was still an intern going on rounds with one of New York's most illustrious surgeons, whose name Burrill tactfully chose not to reveal, the great man stopped for a moment at the bed of one patient, examined him briefly, dismissed the case as "chronic appendicitis–nothing new!" and passed to the next bed with the attending interns and other staff following. "But," Burrill recalled, "something about the case aroused my doubts, and I went back to examine the man's belly. There I saw a faint line of what appeared to be a scar on his stomach from a previous operation and on my inquiring, the patient volunteered the information that his appendix had been removed some years ago, which of course in my mind dispelled any question regarding the fanciful diagnosis of 'chronic appendicitis.' It was a lesson I never forgot."

Burrill and some of his more astute associates were convinced that the fads of colonic irrigation and routine appendix removal accomplished little or nothing, and that these so-called internal medicine specialists should be required to be certified by the American Board of Internal Medicine, which had rigid standards for specialists in the field of gastroenterology. Their views prevailed and gradually these unqualified "specialists," lacking such certification, and accordingly unable to obtain admission to practice as specialists in the better hospitals, were replaced by properly trained specialists in internal medicine.

It took a long time, however, for these fads and fixations on appendix removal and colonic irrigation to be overcome, and only then did the profession begin to think of other diseases which might be the cause of lower abdominal pain.

Another early target of Dr. Crohn and some of his more skeptical confreres was what they regarded as the overuse of intestinal surgery. The sad fact was that in the early days before the First World War, even qualified specialists in internal medicine knew almost nothing about ileitis, ulcerative colitis and diverticulitis. These diseases of the stomach and intestines were not yet recognized. In almost all cases when a patient complained of stomach distress which did not respond to the very limited drugs then available, the only answer was to perform a gastroenterostomy, the surgical removal of part of the intestine. Due to the still primitive state of x-ray methods, diagnosis of stomach and intestinal problems could not be made with any certainty. Instead, the history of the patient, palpation of the abdomen and deduction were relied on, and if the pain was not relieved a gastroenterostomy was performed.

Burrill and his associates analyzed the results of all these surgical operations, found the results very disappointing, and engaged in a determined endeavor to discourage them. This was nothing less than heresy and there was widespread criticism of the dissidents. However, it happened that Dr. William J. Mayo of the famous Mayo Clinic paid a visit to Mount Sinai, discussed the findings of Burrill and his friends and was deeply impressed. As a result Burrill was invited by the American Gastroenterological Association to deliver a paper embodying his and his associates findings, and was greeted with a rising vote of thanks. A year later, in 1917, Burrill was made a member of the association, never thereafter missed one of their meetings and was elected its president in 1933.

The Discovery of Regional Ileitis (Crohn's Disease)

In 1929, a young man seventeen years old was admitted as a patient to Mount Sinai hospital with inflammation of the small bowel, a large mass in the abdomen, diarrhea and severe pain. At this time, all internists routinely assumed that inflammation of the small intestine was due to tuberculosis which was then rampant, and that intestinal tuberculosis was the last stage for which no promising medical treatment existed, and accordingly the patient was discharged. During the next two years the young man was readmitted three more times with the same symptoms and the same diagnosis.

In 1931, when he was admitted for the fourth time, Burrill didn't know how to treat him except by removing the lower part of the stomach and the ulcer, but no surgeon was willing to operate. Finally, he persuaded his colleague, the famous A.A. Berg, to do so. The mass was removed and the operation was a success. When the mass removed from the patient was examined in the laboratory by Burrill and two of his associates, Dr. Leon Ginsberg and Dr. Gordon Oppenheimer, tuberculosis was ruled out and the result was the discovery of a new disease–regional ileitis, an inflammation of the intestinal tract, once thought to be a form of tuberculosis, which surgeons and the medical profession had overlooked all these years and which was cured by a relatively simple operation.

The findings, contained in a paper read before the May 1932 meeting of the American Gastroenterological Association, created a sensation. The new disease was thereafter accepted throughout the medical world and given the name "Crohn's Disease." Within a year or two many more cases of regional ileitis were found. As many as twenty-five percent of these cases had been incorrectly diagnosed in the past as so-called "chronic appendicitis," a non-existent disease. "Had the surgeons been slightly more inquisitive," Burrill was to observe, "and had they, instead of removing the innocent appendix, let their fingers glide over to the small intestine immediately adjacent, they would have felt the characteristic mass."

Another innovation in the treatment of peptic ulcers which was introduced by Dr. Crohn and his associates, who for some time had expressed cautious disapproval of the orthodox method of operating on ulcers, was greeted at first with a storm of disapproval. Their proposal, a new operation to remove part of the stomach and the ulcer was soon adopted as standard practice for operating on peptic ulcers.

A second disease discovered by Dr. Crohn some years later in 1938, was an unusual type of ulcerative colitis, to which an International Medical Congress at Prague gave the name of "Crohn's Disease of the Colon."

Burrill once estimated that in almost sixty years of private practice he had treated 11,000-12,000 cases of regional ileitis and at least 3,000-4,000 cases of ulcerative colitis, with patients referred to him from all over the world.

Late in life, when asked about his judgment that the medical profession had been remiss in failing to discover for so many years such obvious diseases as regional ileitis and ulcerative colitis, he conceded that perhaps they were not actually overlooked; but rather that their failure to be detected may have been the result of ecological changes in our surroundings, and stress, anxiety and neuroses causing intestinal and gastric disorder, rather than actual gastric diseases.

In Insatiable Curiosity

Everything seemed to interest Dr. Crohn. Skeptical of orthodox medical wisdom and many accepted theories and practices, he insisted on testing their validity in the laboratory. One of his early interests was the diagnosis of the functional activity of the pancreatic gland. His friend, Dr. Max Einhorn, had fashioned a rubber tube about three feet long, which could easily be inserted through the nose or down the throat into the stomach and intestines, and the other end used to suck out intestinal secretions for study in the laboratory to see what they were like in normal people. However it was a very uncomfortable procedure to say the least, and Burrill didn't have the heart to subject hospital patients to this ordeal in the interest of science.

What better normal person to experiment on than Burrill himself? So every night he would swallow the three-foot rubber tube, drink a glass of milk to stimulate pancreatic secretion, go to sleep, in the morning o suck out the secretions from the intestine and in the afternoon test them in the laboratory. The result was the publication by him of a number of studies of these secretions as the cause of diseases of the gallbladder, liver, pancreas and other organs.

Halitosis or bad breath was generally believed at the time to be due to decayed teeth, infected tonsils, obstructed nasal passages, and mouth or nasal deviations. After persuading the Bristol Myers Company, a major pharmaceutical firm, to give him a small grant to see if this was true, he proceeded to demonstrate that it was fallacious. His experiments proved that if a person

117

chewed garlic or onions without swallowing them, a few minutes later the odoriferous material could not be detected on his breath. On the other hand, if the same food was digested and absorbed into the blood stream where it was eventually metabolized and reached the lungs, hours later the overpowering odor was expelled in the breath. Burrill tried the experiment on himself with whiskey with the same result. He found that if he gargled with scotch for three minutes and spat it out, the smell couldn't be detected. But if he drank eight ounces at night and went to bed, the next morning his associates were convinced that he had been on an all-night binge.

Another area of interest was too rapid weight loss. He was sharply critical of the hordes of women who flocked to expensive dietary retreats in an effort to acquire slim, girlish figures in a week or two, At the International Congress of Gastroenterology in 1958, he presented a paper on the possibly disastrous effects of this fad, warning that serious illness could result from ill-advised maximum reduction of diet over a short period. He maintained that weight reduction of more than three pounds the first week and two pounds a week thereafter could have seriously harmful results.

Still another shibboleth ridiculed by Dr. Crohn was the so-called medical wisdom of the need for daily bowel movement. "Millions of people," he noted, "consider this the sine qua non for happiness." Before the Pure Food and Drug Act there was a positive mania for Lydia Pinkham's Pink Pills for Pale Ladies and other nostrums guaranteeing to cure constipation. This was utter nonsense. Many people could go for days or even a week without relieving themselves, he pointed out. "There is nothing in the Constitution of the United States," Burrill said, "that guarantees the right to a daily bowel movement!" Habitual constipation, he added, was due to poor exercise, irregular habits and lack of roughage in diets.

Finally, he saw the importance of the extent to which people varied in the extent to which they were sensitive to pain. The susceptibility of people to physical pain differed enormously from one person to another. Burrill himself was almost totally pain insensitive. He could allow a dentist to extract one of his teeth with a forceps without even local anesthesia. He realized this could be a matter of vital importance in the treatment of patients with ulcers and other serious stomach illnesses. Eighty percent of patients with ulcers were pain insensitive. Such persons could have sudden serious gross hemorrhages of the stomach which could prove fatal. Moreover, other pain insensitive persons could be suffering from life threatening stomach illnesses without being aware of it. He devised a simple test for measuring sensitivity to pain by pressing firmly on the area behind the ear back of the mastoid.

On the Witness Stand

He was a constant and acerbic critic of false and exaggerated claims of pharmaceutical and drug companies for their products. As a result, he was frequently called upon by the government to testify before the Federal Trade Commission on the validity and accuracy of these claims. His testimony that Carter's

Little Liver Pills had no ingredients that could have an appreciable effect on the liver resulted in the omission of the work "liver" from their slogan. In another case he helped in the successful prosecution of a manufacturer of vitamins for claiming sensational health cures for what Dr. Crohn termed a ridiculously low dosage of vitamins.

Unfortunately however, Burrill felt that notwithstanding the impressive efforts made and funds spent by the Federal Trade Commission, far too many false advertising claims of the drug industry were never successfully prosecuted.

What to Tell Terminally Ill Patients

The problem of candor on the part of the doctor with patients suffering from serious illness, especially with terminal cancer, always troubled Dr. Crohn, as it did so many physicians. Few people, he claimed, can take even a guarded or discouraging diagnosis with equanimity. The slightest hesitation on the part of the physician, a doubtful look on his face, may throw the patient into a panic, particularly when the possibility of malignancy exists. Consequently, although he agreed that the members of the family or close relatives must be told, the patient himself should usually be left in ignorance if possible. Only the strongest minds or those endowed with great religious faith will accept the verdict that death is inevitable; and he recalled only two patients during his long career in that category–a Jesuit priest and an orthodox Jewish rabbi.

The priest had received the last rites of the Church and knew his end was near. "The rabbi," Burrill recalled, "was a Talmudic scholar, fully bearded, his face wrinkled with care. Whenever one entered his room, he had his Book of Psalms on his lap, silently reading. One day when I visited him, he ceased praying and looked up. 'Doctor, shall I die?' he asked. I hesitated a moment, feeling that this philosophical man truly wanted to know his destiny and make his peace with his Maker. Then I nodded and replied 'Yes.' He gazed at me for a moment and his eyes dropped, but there was no change in his countenance. Then he resumed reading the Psalms of David."

Burrill himself, while in his eighties, endured two operations for cancer of the colon. It never slowed him down or dampened his spirits or enthusiasm. The only cure for cancer, he claimed, was early detection.

Bachelorhood and Remarriage

Burrill was forty-three at the time of his divorce in 1927. By prior arrangement, he lived with his daughter Ruth while his son Edward lived with Edward's mother. For several years father and daughter lived in an apartment with Burrill's now widowed father, Theodore; and thereafter in larger quarters with not only Theodore, but with Burrill's brother Josh and Aunt Mallie Baum. Finally, when Ruth was sixteen, she moved with him into their own apartment at 88th Street and Riverside Drive.

Still an attractive, vigorous man, there was never any question of Burrill's living the life of a celibate. His personal charm, keen intellect and lively interest in music, painting and literature continuously brought him into contact with women having similar tastes. His daughter Ruth, while understandably reticent about discussing the identity of her father's female companions during this period, nevertheless confided that there were many of them.

Meanwhile, Ruth had married Gerald Dickler; and in the spring of 1947 the young couple refurbished for a vacation home a small hundred-year-old house in New Milford, Connecticut, which they purchased from Rose Elbogen, a lady who lived with her husband about a mile away. The Dicklers and Burrill worked like beavers all summer, collecting flat rocks picked up here and there from old stone walls in the area, added a large stone terrace, damned the stream and cultivated the hillside.

A few months later in October, their neighbor Paul Elbogen died quite suddenly and Rose, a charming and very attractive woman, was left a sad widow. Dr. Crohn climbed up the long hill to pay a condolence call, returned the following day, and like "The Man Who Came to Dinner," stayed. He courted Rose all that winter and the following summer they were married.

The ceremony took place one June day in a courtroom in the Bronx, with New York City Municipal Judge Martin Frank, a patient of Dr. Crohn, officiating. Ruth and her brother Edward, together with Ruth's husband Gerry Dickler, were seated in the back of the courtroom with Burrill and Rose, waiting for the judge to dispose of his last case. "Finally," Ruth recalled, "the judge called Burrill to the bench, and there ensued an inordinately lengthy conversation between the two.

Gerry, a lawyer, who had prepared all the divorce papers ahead of time and sent them to the judge, began to get terribly nervous as the conversation between the two at the bench dragged on and on. Could there have been some terrible legal oversight on Gerry's part that would prevent the marriage from taking place?

"Eventually, the judge signaled and we all trooped to the bench for the ceremony, and after it was performed we all left the courtroom. Gerry could hardly wait.

"'What in the world were you talking about all that time with the judge?' he asked. "Oh,' responded Dad, 'we were discussing his ulcer.'"

Burrill was sixty-four years old, and Rose at first was somewhat uneasy at the difference in their ages; but Burrill still so active, enthusiastic and full of physical energy, overcame whatever misgivings she had. It turned out to be a wonderfully successful marriage. Rose, like Burrill, was cultured, active, artistic and musical, a trustee of the Berkshire Foundation dedicated to helping young musicians. Sharing the same interests they led an active social life, and much the next thirty-five years of their marriage was spent traveling to all corners of the globe. Rose confessed that she, like so many others, had difficulty keeping up with him.

In 1949, at the age of sixty-five, Burrill was required under the hospital's rules to retire from ward service at Mount Sinai. Thereafter all his medical activity was devoted to his now lucrative and scientifically stimulating private practice, and to lecturing and attending medical meetings and conferences all over the world.

President Eisenhower's Illness

One hot summer day in June 1956, while Dr. Crohn was at his country home in New Milford planting corn, the news suddenly came blaring over the radio that President Eisenhower was ill and was to be operated on for an intestinal obstruction due to regional ileitis or Crohn's disease. immediately the telephone started ringing with calls from newspapermen from all over the country.

"The editor of *The Washington Post*," recalled Burrill, "was on the phone. The New York Academy of Medicine had been contacted and referred all calls to me. What did I think of the President's chances? Would he survive? Would he be well? Taken utterly by surprise and not being in possession of any of the salient facts in the case, this required some fast thinking.

"I knew that three weeks earlier the President had been thoroughly examined, including complete x-rays of the intestinal tract and found to be in good health. I knew also that obstruction in ileitis is a late manifestation of the disease, occurring during the healing process and caused by a growth of scar tissue in the intestinal tract. However, I told the press that a by-passing operation was all that was necessary to relieve the obstruction, which could be performed without endangering his life and probably would be curative."

The statement was instantly repeated word for word on the Wall Street ticker tape and broadcast around the world. Almost immediately the stock market, which had fallen precipitously with the news of the President's illness, quickly rebounded to the tune of $2 million in increased volume. For the next few weeks, Burrill, now an international celebrity, received dozens of invitations to appear on "Meet the Press," and other special TV and radio programs to discuss the Eisenhower case, all of which he politely declined.

Round the World Trip

Frederick March, the celebrated moving picture actor and his wife, the actress Florence Eldridge, were neighbors of Burrill and Rose in New Milford. They met frequently at community affairs, were attracted to one another and had become close friends. In 1960 they embarked on a four-month trip around the world together that would take them to Israel, Iran, India, Singapore, Indonesia, Bali, Ceylon, Hong Kong, Taiwan and Japan.

For the Crohns, this like their other excursions abroad in subsequent years, was no luxurious, comfortable, conventional trip to the familiar, well-known places and sights favored by typical tourists. Rather, they with their keen interest in ancient history, exotic art and the culture of strange civilizations, sought out in addition, the unusual out of the way places and remote archaeological sites. Moreover, being in the company of a world-famous acting couple resulted in their being invited to be guests of the Maharajah of Mysore, the Maharajah of Jaipur and other notables.

Burrill Crohn as Geologist

One petty but exceedingly annoying incident occurred near Madras in India, when at the border of two provinces their belongings were searched by the local police, who discovered that Dr. Crohn's medicine bag contained four ounces of scotch whiskey, kept for a possible emergency. All four were detained and Burrill was threatened with criminal prosecution for violating a local ordinance against carrying liquor; and it took twenty-four hours of frantic telephone calls, including one by Mr. March to Prime Minister Nehru, before the misunderstanding which made headlines in the world press was cleared up. It is ironical that in India, where boys of nine or ten were routinely sold by their parents into virtual bondage for life to carpet weavers, and untouchables were the victims of the cruelest discrimination, that an American doctor should have been arrested for possessing a few ounces of whiskey for medicinal purposes.

Wherever they went, in Israel, Iran, Bombay, New Delhi and elsewhere, Dr. Crohn was invited to address the leading association of physicians and medical school. "It was 105 degrees Fahrenheit outside," Burrill wrote, when he addressed the medical school of the University of Cairo. "The hall was not air-conditioned, there was no loud speaker, and the drinking water in the carafe looked as if it had come from the Nile and was obviously impotable. My only suit was clinging to me long before the end of my lecture." But afterward he was offered a three months honorary professorship in Egypt, which he graciously declined–quite an honor, extended as it was to an American Jewish doctor by a country which at the time was still in a state of war with the State of Israel.

On another occasion while wandering through the medieval streets of Salamanca in Spain, they visited the university founded in the 12th century and its medical school, one of the first in Europe. The result was a cordial invitation to return the next day to address the student body. No plea of lack of preparation, lack of slides or illustrations was acceptable. The next morning for an hour in a crowded auditorium, with a piece of chalk, a blackboard and an eraser, interrupted by an interpreter, Burrill elucidated the subject of regional ileitis (Crohn's Disease) to a rapt audience.

In 1969, hoping to devote all of his time to his Connecticut farm, and to enjoying retirement with his wife, Dr. Crohn sent out a retirement notice, borrowing the following sentiments from the words of Thomas Jefferson when he retired from public life:

> "The motion of my blood no longer keeps time with the tumult of the world. It leads me to seek for happiness in the lap of, and love of, my family, in the society of my neighbors and my books, in the wholesome occupation of my farm and my affairs, in the interest and affection for every kind of bud that opens, in every breath that blows around me, owing account to myself alone of my hours and actions."

However, his patients refused to believe him, and he was obliged to continue his private practice, limiting it to three mornings a week, with long vacations in the summer and short holidays at other times of the year.

Expert in the City's History

Always an enthusiastic New Yorker, he loved the variety of its neighborhoods, the diversity of its population, its innumerable landmarks, monuments and places of historic interest. In 1970, an incident occurred which was the subject of an article about him in *Reader's Digest*, which gives a good idea of this aspect of Burrill's personality. One day, seeing a bus approaching 84th Street and Fifth Avenue outside his apartment, he first flagged it down, and then started to back away when he saw that it was a chartered sightseeing tour bus.

"Graciously," the article went on, "the tour conductor invited the distinguished man aboard, and then continued with his spiel:

"'This is where Jacqueline Onassis lives . . . and here is where the husband of the late Judy Garland pays $100 a day for a room . . .

"'Don't forget to tell them,' Burrill broke in, 'that the place next door belonged to Charles Fletcher, who made a fortune selling Castoria, and that pretty soon we will be coming to a gem of a museum built by Henry Clay Frick with the help of Andrew Carnegie.'

"At this, the tour conductor turned his megaphone over to his guest. For the next ten blocks Dr. Crohn told his audience how, as a boy, he played on upper Madison Avenue when goats still roamed the streets, how he carried a tin pail over to a farm (now Sutton Place) for milk, how his mother told him about watching Lincoln's funeral cortege pass through these streets when she was a girl.

"When the bus let him off at his stopping point, the passengers cheered him.

"'I think they were sorry to see me go,' Burrill told his wife that night; 'the tour director was leaving out too much.'"

Honors Received and Tributes to His Contemporaries

In addition to serving as President of the American Gastroenterological Association in 1932, Burrill was awarded that organization's Julius Friedanthal Medal in 1953. He was Honorary President of the International Congress of Gastroenterology, was made Emeritus Professor of Medicine at the Mount Sinai Medical School, and among other awards, received the Silver Medal from the College of Physicians and Surgeons of Columbia University. In addition, he wrote five books, including *Affections of the Stomach* in 1927 and *Understand Your Ulcer* in 1950, as well as over 150 published medical articles and studies.

He rubbed shoulders with virtually all the prominent figures in internal medicine during the better part of the twentieth century and knew many of them intimately. In spite of all the honors bestowed on him he remained a man of extreme modesty and was generous in praise of his medical contemporaries.

Of Dr. Emanuel Libman, his chief at Mount Sinai Hospital, he described this incident illustrating Dr. Libman's extraordinary intuition in the diagnosis of disease:

"A well-to-do family had arranged for a consultation by a group of eminent doctors, including Dr. Libman, to examine their seriously ill child at their Fifth Avenue mansion. The group of doctors, none of which had ever seen the patient, much less made a diagnosis, were assembled in the downstairs entrance hall preparing to ascend to the bedroom where the child lay. As the group started to ascend the broad marble staircase, a short sharp cough was heard from the patient's room. 'Ah,' said Dr. Libman, 'I see or rather hear that we have another case of meningitis.'"

In the early days of the century, speed in performing surgery, Burrill recalled, was vital because anesthesia were so crude that the operation had to be completed quickly, before the patient "woke up." His friend, Dr. A.A. Berg, Burrill said, "was brave, venturesome and capable of surgery that nobody else would tackle, operating quickly with a very fine technique." Burrill's associate, Dr. Ralph Colp of Mount Sinai, was another brilliant surgeon who operated rapidly. Burrill had made an arrangement with Dr. Colp for the removal of the appendix of one of Burrill's patients, the operation to start at 1:30 P.M. "I arrived at the hospital at twenty-five minutes to two and found him sewing up a patient. 'When are you going to operate on my case?' I said. 'I just finished,' he replied. I said, 'But you scheduled it for 1:30!' 'That's right,' he replied. 'I started at 1:30 and now I'm sewing him up.'"

A Critic of Excessive Medical Research

Although he himself had devoted much of his life to research and laboratory work, toward the end of his career Burrill felt that research was being overdone. While conceding that without it mankind would never have had the benefit of Fleming's discovery of penicillin in 1929, and other medical milestones, he maintained that too much time and money were being spent on medical research to the detriment of clinical medicine. Much of the too generous research grants of the

National Institute of Health, and untold millions spent by hundreds of the nation's hospitals and teaching institutions was being wasted on repetitious abstruse and unessential papers and studies with respect to matters long since settled, most of which went into waste-baskets.

"Our hospital beds," he complained, "are over-crowded with patients sent by doctors for so-called studies or tests ad nauseam, all financed by federal and state governments through Medicare or Medicaid, with the result that really sick and even emergency patients can't be admitted to hospitals for lack of beds."

Other Interests

Despite a career in medicine and medical research spanning some sixty-five years, Burrill somehow found time to indulge an extraordinarily wide range of other interests. A man of enormous physical and mental energy, he and his wife Rose did carpentry, dug in the earth, planted seeds for corn and other vegetables and harvested a large garden.

Always a lover of classical music, he later developed through his first wife an interest in painting and sculpture. His own water colors were exhibited each year at the New Milford art shows.

His favorite reading was Roman, English and American history. Paraphrasing Chekhov, he liked to say, "Medicine is my lawful wife, and history is my mistress."

Burrill

He was also a Civil War buff. "Since childhood," he wrote, "when I watched the Zouaves and the Grand Army of the Republic march down Fifth Avenue on Decoration Day, the history of the Civil War has engaged my interest." While reviewing the history of Mount Sinai Hospital, he discovered that one Israel Moses, its first appointed surgeon in 1859, became a lieutenant colonel when the Civil War began, organized his own regiment and joined the army of General George McClellan and fought in the Peninsula campaign. Later he joined the Army Medical Corps and turned out to be the physician who accompanied the crazy army contingent that tried unsuccessfully to overthrow the government of Nicaragua. Burrill wrote a monograph about him: "Dr. Israel Moses, Surgeon" in 1944.

"He was an interesting character," was Burrill's wry comment.

Patients

Burrill joked that when he first started private practice as a young doctor, his patients were mostly his brothers and sisters, all ten of them, and their offspring. As his reputation and practice grew, his patients came to him from all corners of the world, from South America, Europe, and the Far East. Some of them provided interesting anecdotes.

"Mrs. Luria, a Jewish widow immigrant from Hungary, called one day in great excitement, claiming that she was going to have a stroke. When I arrived at her home I found out that her

134

high fever was due to the fact that her son had informed her that he was going to marry a gentile girl. I ordered her to remain in bed and called the Nurses Registry for a twenty-four hour private nurse. When the nurse, a young woman by the name O'Connor, arrived, I gave her explicit instructions not to discuss the patient's problem with her.

"When I came the next day for my daily visit at two o'clock in the afternoon, the nurse was gone for her customary two-hour rest period. I entered the bedroom and found Mrs. Luria weeping uncontrollably.

"'Mrs. Luria,' I said, 'this is your doctor.' But she refused to talk to me. Finally she turned around, faced me and shrieked: 'That was a fine nurse you sent to take care of me!'

"'What did she do?'

"'She spent the whole night telling me about _her_ problem. She's engaged to a rabbi's son and the rabbi refuses to give his consent!'"

Another patient, a nephew of Bernard Berenson, the internationally known art critic and historian, hearing that Dr. Crohn and his wife were going on a trip to Italy, asked him while in Florence to visit his uncle, who was suffering from stomach distress. Burrill agreed to do so and on arriving in Florence made arrangements to visit the great man, who lived in a magnificent villa on the outskirts of the city in relative solitude.

In preparing his examination, two servants undressed him and carried him to his bed.

"I examined him and found nothing seriously wrong, gave him some samples of mild medicine that he could take, and promised to send him more, and for years thereafter continued to do so. He was very appreciative and took us to a room containing his own special collection of Siennese art, and then to his library, a huge room stacked to the ceiling with art reference books. Since I considered myself somewhat knowledgeable about art, I ventured to refer to a certain French Impressionist painting as the work of a particular artist. With charming politeness, he corrected me as to the painter's name and calling for one of his assistants to bring him a ladder, climbed and retrieved a certain volume on the top shelf, opened it at the proper page and showed me my mistake.

"Afterward, as a sign of appreciation for my visit, we were served a light lunch and taken by him on a tour of his magnificent gardens, which I later learned he did only for special guests."

Most patients were grateful for Burrill's services, but not all. Late one evening he received an urgent request to travel to a hospital in Brooklyn for a consultation. Arriving there well past midnight, he was told that the patient, a young woman, had just returned from a holiday in Mexico, where she had apparently eaten tainted food and was suffering from hepatitis (inflammation of the liver), was semi-comatose, deep yellow in color and with a high fever.

"She was obviously on the point of death," Burrill recalled. "The family had been notified that there was no hope and my visit was simply to back up the staff and assure the family that everything known to science had been done."

"Suddenly it occurred to me that there was a form of malaria which at that time was rife in Mexico, which was so severe as to cause fatal hepatitis. I quickly had one of the staff prick her finger and test her blood specimen for malaria plasmodea, and, sure enough her blood was teeming with it. Immediately an intravenous dose of quinine was given and the next morning she was sitting up in bed eating her breakfast with gusto. But when I submitted my bill of fifty dollars for my midnight visit, the family protested that I was overcharging them."

Another time, Dr. Crohn treated a ward patient suffering from pneumonia with great solicitude and care until the critical stage of his illness had passed and he was well on the way to recovery. After a two-week period of convalescence, he was discharged. Dr. Crohn happened to be standing on the steps of the hospital when he spotted the man, now in his street clothes as he was about to leave. "I was delighted to see him now able to leave the hospital fully recovered and smiled at him. But he passed me by without even a word of recognition. I was annoyed and tapped him on the shoulder and said, 'Mister, you might at least say hello. You know, I saved your life!'

"'You didn't do it, God did!' he replied. He was probably right, Burrill reflected–God, or natural curative forces, or such therapeutic science as we had at the time.

Then there were the patients who never let you alone, whom no answer would satisfy. One night, he was awakened at midnight by a very agitated voice claiming her husband was terribly upset because he couldn't sleep.

"I prescribed a simple remedy. Half an hour later, she called again. 'Doctor, the pills haven't helped. Can you suggest something else?' Dead tired and annoyed at the triviality of the complaint, I told her to give him some whiskey and turned over and went back to sleep.

"Five minutes later she was on the phone again! 'How much whiskey?' 'An ounce,' I responded.

"Just as I was getting back to sleep for the fourth time, the phone rang again.

"'Doctor, scotch or rye?'"

Birthday Parties

A man like Burrill, so full of physical vigor and zest for life didn't regard himself as really old, even as he reached the age when most other men were starting to deteriorate physically and mentally. One Sunday morning around the time of his seventy-fifth birthday, he and his son-in-law Gerry Dickler were walking on Madison Avenue when a very attractive matron passed on the other side of the street. Burrill turned his head, sighed, and said, "Oh, to be sixty-five again!"

As the years passed, these birthdays, especially his eighty-fifth and ninety-fifth, were the occasion for large family parties attended not only by his own children, grandchildren and great-grandchildren, but by his brothers and sisters and their large families and other surviving members of the large Baum-Crohn-Webster clan. Needless to say, there were songs, comic skits and other entertainment centered around Burrill's foibles and eccentricities.

On June 13, 1959, at his seventy-fifth birthday party, the ribbing included a series of fictitious Western Union telegrams, each addressed to Dr. Burrill S. Crohn, RFD South Kent Connecticut, including the following:

From the U.S. Department of Agriculture:
"HAVEN'T WE ENOUGH SURPLUS CROPS WITHOUT YOU ADDING TO OUR PROBLEMS. STOP PLANTING NOW"

Ezra Taft Benson, Sec'y of Agriculture

From the World Champion Bridge Expert:
"I KNOW BEAUTIFUL BLONDE AVAILABLE ONLY MONDAY NIGHT. WILL YOU GIVE UP BRIDGE FOR HER? CAN YOU FINESSE?"

Charles Goren

From the White House:
"I HAVE JUST BEEN INFORMED THAT I HAD CROHN'S DISEASE. I THOUGHT IT WAS JUST ILEITIS. I AM DEEPLY INDEBTED TO YOU FOR DISCOVERING SOMETHING WHICH I COULD RECOVER FROM. IT IS MUCH BETTER THAN DEMOCRATS. HAVE YOU A CURE FOR THEM? CONGRATULATIONS ON YOUR BIRTHDAY. I'M GETTING ON TOO."

Ike Eisenhower

From London, England:
"MUST YOU PAINT TOO? LOOK WHAT HAPPENED TO HITLER."

Winston Churchill

From Little Rock, Arkansas:
"DON'T YOU KNOW THE CIVIL WAR IS OVER?"

Orvil Faubus (ex-Governor)

At his eighty-fifth birthday party, his daughter Ruth Dickler wrote that all the manifold and varied activities of this painter, history buff, music lover, world traveler, "this tiller of the soil who extracts prodigious amounts of crab grass without disturbing other weeds, this charter member of the Monday Night Bridge Club, which has been the principle source of support for generations of indigent, needy, and I might add, indifferent bridge players, have all been carried out in his spare time, of which he has none."

He was in his nineties when I and my wife found that we and my cousin Burrill and his wife, Rose, were attending a series of Chamber Music Society concerts at Lincoln Center on the same nights. During the intermission, I would go over and sit down next to Burrill and chat with him. Each time, he would greet me with the greatest pleasure, and would start to reminisce about the days of his youth, when he and my father Cecil would walk back and forth downtown to City College to save carfare, only to gamble away their savings at the Saturday night poker game at the home of their Webster cousins. At the conclusion of the last concert that spring, he and Rose and I and my wife stopped to say goodnight to one another in the lobby. It was raining and the Crohns were intent on catching a cab on the corner. Opening his umbrella and taking Rose by the arm, the two of them turned around, waved goodbye to us, and looking like a couple half their age, briskly trotted off to the corner. That was the last time I saw him.

He died in his one-hundredth year on July 23, 1983, at his country home in Merryall Connecticut.

He was often asked: "How do you account for your long life, your unusual energy and your excellent health?"

To this he replied: "I can only say that I attribute my vigorous health to a physical and mental restlessness and constant state of curiosity, as well as to the splendid genes and chromosomes inherited from my parents."

CHAPTER IV

THE SCHOOL TEACHERS

During the latter part of the last century, from about 1880 to the end of World War I and even thereafter, the employment prospects of young educated American women were very limited. In theory, the medical, legal, accounting and other skilled professions were open to them but, in fact opportunities in these fields were severely restricted.

While there were a number of separate medical schools for women and the leading medical schools for men finally started to admit women around 1890, women doctors in operating rooms, hospital laboratories and dissecting rooms were all but unheard of. Clinical appointments, residencies and even internships for women in major hospitals in New York, Boston and elsewhere were scattered and irregular. The American Medical Association was closed to female membership until 1915.

The other professions were equally inhospitable to women. Columbia University Law School did not open its doors to women until 1928, and the New York City Bar Association remained a gentlemen's club until 1937. The leading law and accounting firms accepted no women as associates, much less as partners. Indeed, the accounting profession regarded women as unreliable gossips who could not be trusted to keep confidential the affairs and business secrets of their clients. Needless to say, only low-level office, clerical and stenographic jobs were available to women in the business, industrial and banking world.

In short, with the only other opportunities open to them being jobs as sales girls in department stores, stenographers, clerical workers or nurses, it is not surprising that the young daughters and granddaughters of Abbe and Israel Baum and of Jacob Webster flocked to teaching in New York City's public schools.

Conditions in the City's Public Schools

The situation in the city's public school system toward the end of the last century and thereafter bordered on the chaotic. Boys and girls in most districts attended separate schools or classes. There were no high schools. In the densely populated slums of the lower East Side and other poor districts teeming with new immigrants from Europe, school buildings were in a decrepit state, classrooms and bathrooms were dirty and unsanitary, and truancy and juvenile delinquency were rampant. Classes for the first three years were dangerously over-crowded with as many as eighty-five pupils in one classroom, whereas there were surplus seats in the upper grades due to pupils dropping out for lack of interest or in order to take jobs when they reached the legally permissible working age of fourteen. Conditions in the uptown schools were better, but still critical, with the same antiquated school buildings, over-crowding and lack of seats in the lower forms, two children often sharing the same seat, and a surplus of seats in the upper grades. Teacher training was superficial or non-existent. The promotion of teachers was by seniority and frequently the result of political or personal favoritism rather than due to merit. Women, who greatly outnumbered male teachers, were blatantly discriminated against and were paid less than one-half of what men received for the same job. Until 1904, a woman teacher who married was immediately dismissed.

Worst of all, teaching methods were mechanical and the curriculum archaic. The emphasis was on strict discipline and on memorizing a predetermined body of knowledge–facts, rules, definitions and numbers–and all creativity, independent thinking and imagination were discouraged. Their lack of training contributed to teacher dependence on mechanical methods of teaching, and due to the absence of a merit system for promotion, teachers had little incentive to introduce more progressive methods into the classroom.

The Movement for Reform

The movement for reform of the public schools pitted the forces of "good government," led by wealthier citizens–merchants, bankers and lawyers, for the most part Protestant and Anglo-Saxon, everyone from Nicholas Murray Butler to Theodore Roosevelt, Elihu Root and Charles Evans Hughes–against the Democratic politicians and Tammany Hall. The reformers called for putting more schools in districts suffering from overcrowding; competitive examinations and promotion by a merit system for teachers, with equal pay for men and women; more vocational training; special classes for the handicapped, slow learners and non-English speaking pupils. Above all they pressed for progressive teaching methods and ending the emphasis on memorization.

But the Democrats in Tammany Hall who controlled the city government and the bureaucracy fought every effort to improve matters and, strange to say, most teachers and principals, especially those lacking in training or competence, fearing the merit system and competitive examinations, supported them.

By 1915 considerable improvements were made, including a more centralized school system with greater power in the Board of Education and less power in the local boards, improved teaching standards, the appointment and promotion of teachers on the basis of merit, and equal pay for women teachers. Perhaps most important, the school curriculum was reorganized to conform to progressive education principles together with a vast expansion of vocational training. Still the relentless increase in immigration was such that all the old problems of overcrowding, antiquated school buildings, truancy and large percentages of pupils being over age for their grade or dropping out, remained. By 1930, due to shifts in the population and increased pupil enrollment, there were still 50,000 part-time students, and with the beginning of the Depression, funding for new school facilities was cut, teachers' salaries were reduced and class sizes increased.

However, the advent of the New Deal and the LaGuardia administration in City Hall resulted in new federal programs with funding for additional schools, including nursery schools, adult and remedial education, fast-track programs for high achievers and additional vocational programs for others. By 1940 pupil enrollment had dropped from over 1.4 million to 827,000, due to the fact that the schools no longer had to cope with the overwhelming numbers and social problems of first-generation immigrant children. Of course the formidable new problems which would result from the massive demographic changes due to the huge immigration of blacks from the South and Hispanics from the Caribbean during and after World War II were still to come.

Temporary Employment and Lifetime Careers

With the children and grandchildren of the Baums, Websters and Crohns, teaching in the city's public schools became a family tradition. All one needed to teach school was a primary school education and a college diploma. There were no high schools in those days. One can picture the daughters of Abbe Baum–Millicent, Sarah and Mallie, and Rebecca, the daughter of Abbe's brother Israel–all born a few years after the Civil War, all of them graduates of Hunter College, entering their classrooms, dressed in what was virtually the woman teacher's uniform at the time–skirt down to the ankles, long-sleeved shirtwaist with collar and tie, the hair piled high on the head or rolled in a bun in back. They were followed in due course by Esther Crohn, Naomi Crohn, Jane Webster and Judith Epstein, younger members of the Baum-Webster-Crohn clan, also recent graduates of Hunter. Even some of Abbe Baum's male descendants, Dr. Burrill Crohn the world-famous

Public School Teachers (1890)

Public School 157 (1901)

gastroenterologist and discover of Crohn's Disease, and Joshua Epstein who later spent his business career in advertising, taught public school for a while.

All of them, having grown up in families that put a premium on culture and education, were well equipped to command the attention and interest of youngsters even under the difficult and trying conditions then prevailing in the schools. Needless to say, they refused to be limited to the archaic and mechanical teaching practices then in vogue, and instead adopted the more imaginative and progressive teaching methods which were now in use in the better private schools.

Most of them took temporary teaching jobs in order to support themselves or to contribute to family expenses at home. Sarah Baum was still a young girl of seventeen when she traveled every day by streetcar to Inwood in upper Manhattan where she taught at the local public school. In the historic blizzard of 1888 when she was marooned in a crowded trolley car for twenty-two hours, the vivacious and loquacious Sarah, in spite of the bitter cold and anxiety, kept up the spirits of her fellow passengers with her stories and songs until a rescue squad arrived. She stopped teaching when she married and moved to Worcester, Massachusetts, where she taught English to Jewish immigrants who had settled there.

Esther Crohn, the oldest child of Theodore Crohn, graduated from Hunter College in 1902 and received an appointment to teach at P.S. Number One on Broome Street on the lower East Side.

"The neighborhood," she later recalled, "was unfamiliar, so I asked my father to take me downtown to school the first day. I remember the pushcarts and fish peddlers, because I slipped on the fish scales which fell on the street when they cleaned the fish. The children, whose parents had newly arrived from Europe, spoke very little English. But they loved their teachers and were very eager to learn. I had to take my class to the shower room every Friday afternoon. Each pupil brought his own soap and towel. They had no bathtubs in their homes, only wash tubs, which were filled to the top with coal and wood for the stove. As a substitute teacher I earned the munificent sum of fifty dollars a month."

After her marriage to Ben Shapiro, the couple moved to Far Rockaway and Esther again accepted appointment as a substitute teacher at P.S. 39. Here the children were often wild and disorderly and discipline was poor. One day on entering her classroom she found the boys and girls racing about wildly, leaping on the desks and screaming. Unable to restore order, she went to the principal's office and submitted her resignation.

Other young women of the Baum-Webster-Crohn clan who taught school temporarily or until they were married were Naomi Crohn Esther's younger sister, Jane Webster the daughter of Jacob Webster, and Judith, Sarah Epstein's daughter. Judith left teaching to become an unpaid volunteer with Hadassah, where she rose to world-wide prominence, serving four times as its national president.

Mallie, Millicent and Rebecca Baum

Mallie Baum and Millicent Baum the daughters of Abbe, and another Rebecca, the daughter of Israel Baum, all of them spinsters, made teaching their lifetime careers. Rebecca, "Aunt Becky," was very close to her cousin Mallie with whom she frequently traveled abroad. After retiring from the school system she devoted herself to writing and translating Braille books for the blind.

Mallie and Millicent were both superb teachers widely admired by their associates. Mallie, the younger of the two, taught at P.S. 82 at 70th Street and First Avenue in Yorkville. She was a truly warm, vibrant, exuberant personality. She loved to write original poems, songs and scripts for school plays and ceremonies, as well as for family parties. While these creations were something less than literary or comic masterpieces, they nevertheless exuded extraordinary vitality and genuine feeling. A eulogy to her which appeared in *The New York Times*, stated that "she composed one hundred and fifty school songs in addition to her manifold holiday and graduation skits," and that she had "taught two generations of students in the same family."

No one could understand why, with so much verve and personality, so well-educated and a world traveler, she never married. Apparently it was because she was too finicky. She herself joked that she was waiting for her Prince Charming, "a rich, middle-aged man with a gold watch chain across his middle." Several such suitors actually presented themselves and wanted to marry her, but as her nephew Lawrence Crohn observed, "She was too fastidious to accept them." Ruth Dickler, one of her

Mallie Baum

grand-nieces, recalls how in her later years when she was quite plump, her aunt used to lace up her own corset by tying the ends of the laces to the doorknob and walking briskly away from it. She also remembered Mallie returning from school at the end of the day, her arms loaded with compositions to be read and tests to be graded. What a privilege it was, she said, when her great-aunt would invite her to assist her and entrusted her with correcting batches of papers.

She was very fond of my father Cecil, her nephew, and visited us then in our home on Long Island, making the trip back and forth by railroad, although at that stage in her life, overweight, somewhat red-faced and short of breath, the traveling must not have been easy for her. In fact she had a serious heart condition and died of pneumonia at the age of fifty-five. The family would never forget, observed Lawrence Crohn, "the poignant scene when her young students came to the Crohn apartment where she had been living, and filed silently past her bed where she lay in death."

Millicent Baum was one of the first graduates of Hunter College and, like her sisters, started teaching while in her teens. Her school, at 111th Street near Lexington Avenue, was in a district containing a large Italian immigrant population. Regarded as a first-rate pedagogue, she was promoted year after year and became the school's principal at the age of twenty-eight. Among her famous pupils were the future U.S. Senator Robert F. Wagner and Fiorello LaGuardia, who later became mayor.

She was feisty, dour and crusty and a stern disciplinarian, but nevertheless kindly with her teachers and pupils. Her school was considered a model in the city's school system. Her influence was such that it was a simple matter for her to arrange for two of her young relatives, Burrill Crohn and Joshua Epstein, to obtain teaching jobs which helped them pay their way through college.

Like the rest of the teachers in the family, she abandoned wherever possible the rigid mechanical teaching methods which were still standard in most grammar schools and encouraged her own staff to use the progressive and imaginative ways of teaching which were slowly coming into vogue. A persistent innovator, she persuaded the Board of Education to adopt a number of reforms in the curriculum, including eye examinations and the supplying of eyeglasses for visually handicapped students. She also wrote a training manual for teachers and a primer for young readers.

The Italian neighborhood in her district contained many socialists and other radicals. Although a staunch, life-long Republican, Millicent was a firm believer in the right of free speech, and when a student who espoused socialist principles in a classroom speech was threatened with expulsion, she intervened and forbade it.

After a long career at the 111th Street school, she was placed in charge of the Andrew Draper Junior High School and later was made principal of the first evening high school established in the city, situated in the lower East Side. She never married and lived at home with her mother and sisters until late in life. But she attended national education conferences and seminars all over the country and traveled extensively in Europe every summer.

When she retired at the age of seventy, Fiorello LaGuardia, now the city's mayor, remembered his former teacher and asked her to accept a position as his unofficial Deputy for Public School Education at one dollar a year, installing her in an office next to his own at City Hall, where she served as a trouble-shooter for problems in the school system and as a sort of liaison with the powerful Board of Education. She remained in that office for the next ten years. Every day the mayor sent a city automobile to bring her downtown and to take her home.

She considered herself a cross between a nurse and a bossy mother of the Mayor, constantly upbraiding him for bringing his lunch from home to City Hall in a brown paper bag as being inconsistent with the dignity of his office. LaGuardia was also notoriously indifferent to his dress and appearance. On one occasion reported in the press to an amused public, before a large public meeting at which he was scheduled to speak, the Mayor arrived escorting on his arm Mrs. Eleanor Roosevelt. As they came down the aisle to the front of the hall, Millicent, seated in a front row, jumped out of her seat, rushed up the aisle and hastily adjusted his collar and tie which, as usual, were all askew.

There is a footnote to the story of Millicent, a strange, almost incredible incident revealing another side of her life suppressed and kept secret from all but a few members of the family, which now should be revealed in order to give a true, full picture of the life of this unusual woman.

While still a young school teacher in her early twenties, this bright, personable woman had a sex life unknown to her parents and the rest of her family, including an affair with her brother-in-law, that old reprobate, my grandfather Samuel S. Ruskay, the husband of her sister Esther, which resulted in her pregnancy and the birth of an illegitimate child. When her pregnancy was revealed to her parents Abbe and Goldie Baum, they quietly arranged for her to leave the city for the countryside in upstate New York, where the child was born and a scandal was averted. The child, a boy, was given out for adoption and Millicent resumed her teaching career with no one the wiser. Many years later someone in the family traced the son to the West Coast where he had married and raised a family. Only a few members of the family knew the truth. The incident was never mentioned and in time was almost forgotten; and, strange to say, this severe, domineering, authoritative lady, a prominent, highly respected figure in the public life of the city, was not only revered but became almost a family icon. Indeed new additions to the Baum-Webster-Crohn clan, prospective brides and husbands, were frequently brought before her to be scrutinized. Sylvia Epstein, the widow of David Epstein, remembered that when she became engaged to her husband, he presented her to his great-aunt at a family gathering for her characteristically blunt, almost grudging approval.

She died at the age of eighty-one. The newspapers all carried a prominent article lauding her for her contributions to the city. Mayor LaGuardia closed City Hall for the day and delivered a touching eulogy at her funeral. In addition to praising her for her years of service in the public school system, the Mayor

Millicent Baum conferring with Mayor LaGuardia

referred to the ethical and moral principles instilled in her by her father Abbe Baum.

"Millicent," he said, "was heir to the finest instincts to be found in human beings. She once told me a story about her father's overcoat. The family had saved money for a brand new overcoat for their father. But they never saw him wear it. When queried he said, a new immigrant came to synagogue without a coat. I invited him home and gave him my new one. How could I have given him the old one?'"

CHAPTER V

THE EPSTEINS

Uncle Eddie and Aunt Sarah

The daughters of Abbe Baum were blessed with many admirable qualities, including intelligence and personal warmth. However pulchritude was not among them. Indeed, from any conventional point of view they were quite plain, which perhaps explains why three of them remained spinsters.

So when popular, vivacious Sarah became of marriageable age and no suitor satisfactory to her or her father had presented himself, Abbe decided to take matters into his own hands and engage the services of a marriage broker, a not uncommon practice in the New York Jewish community toward the end of the last century. The result was that some weeks later a quiet, reserved gentleman, Edward Epstein from Worcester, Massachusetts, came to the Baum home and asked Abbe for his daughter's hand in marriage. As Abbe's grandson Lawrence Crohn later noted, "Here was a son-in-law to warm the heart of her father, a learned man, a Talmud scholar, a true Litvak (Lithuanian) and a businessman as well." Although he had one drawback–he spoke English poorly and with a foreign accent–he was tall, handsome, a man of great dignity and integrity.

They were married in 1894, and "Uncle Eddie," as he became known in the family, took his bride back to

Worcester, where he and his brother, having emigrated from a small town in Lithuania when they were young boys, were in the business of manufacturing mens and boys trousers. Sarah soon found out she was the only woman of her generation in the little Jewish community that spoke English and, being a former public school teacher, she started classes in English and American history for her women neighbors. As for Uncle Eddie, she insisted that he go to night school to improve his English. He did so well that, thereafter, although he spoke slowly and with deliberation, most people assumed he was native born.

Their first child, Judith, was born in Worcester, and three years later they decided to move back to New York City, making their home at Lexington Avenue and 95th Street. Uncle Eddie continued in the pants business with a new partner who, a few years later with the firm losing money and without Eddie's knowledge, set their factory on fire to collect the insurance. Honest man that he was, Eddie declined to take advantage of the bankruptcy laws and insisted on paying back the creditors in full, although it took him several years to do so. He continued to manufacture pants on his own with considerable success; and for years thereafter, whenever the numerous growing boys in the Baum, Crohn and Webster households needed new trousers, their mothers would herd them down to Uncle Eddie's factory for replacements.

The Epsteins also had two boys, Josh, named for an uncle, and Abbe, named after Sarah's father. Almost as soon as they could walk, their intensely religious father insisted that they attend Hebrew school three afternoons each week after public school. Although they loved and respected their father, the boys never forgave him for this. Later in life Abbe used to bewail the memory of those long, tedious afternoons which he regarded as a total waste of time. He was a good tennis player and he insisted he might have become a professional had all those innumerable hours in Hebrew school been spent on the tennis court. Uncle Eddie's granddaughter Naomi, on the other hand, who perfected her Hebrew in Palestine where she spent a year at school, fondly recalled the wonderful hours spent with her grandfather studying the works of Bialik, Maimonides and other great Jewish writers.

Uncle Eddie became active in the Kehilah Jeshurin Synagogue on 85th Street and helped establish the Central Jewish Institute, which was nearby. Meanwhile Sarah, a virtual dynamo, threw herself into New York Jewish affairs. She became one of a small group of women who, following the lead of Henrietta Szold, helped found Hadassah, the Women's Zionist Organization of America, in 1913. She was also the founder of the Women's League of the United Synagogue of America and became its president, headed the Women's Division of the Jewish Education Committee and was active in a number of other organizations, including the sisterhood of her synagogue. As if this were not enough, she was well past middle age when she resolved to improve her knowledge of Jewish history and theology and joined the first class of the Teacher's Institute of the Jewish Theological Seminary with Professor Mordecai Kaplan as her teacher.

She was a good public speaker, much in demand, interlarding serious messages with humorous personal anecdotes. "There was always a warm spiritual quality that glowed through her personality," her grandson recalled. She was not easily discouraged. In the midst of World War II, when her daughter Judith was national president of Hadassah and Judith's son David was with the army in France, a cable was received one morning from the War Department, notifying the family that David had been taken prisoner by the Germans during the Battle of the Bulge. Judith, who was scheduled to speak that afternoon at an important press conference, asked her mother whether she should go through with it. "Such a question!" was the reply, "I'm going to speak at my meeting and you will speak at yours!"

In 1929 Eddie and Sarah made their first trip to Palestine and enjoyed it so much that they returned to stay a full year in 1932, at which time Judith and her two children joined them. On the return trip to the United States Eddie and Sarah stopped over for a few days in London. While out walking by himself, Eddie crossed a busy street to buy something at a chemist's shop and, confused by the traffic, was run down by an automobile and killed instantly. All alone and devastated by the tragedy, Sarah bravely endured the pain and grief of accompanying her husband's body back to New York.

He was buried in the cemetery plot he had insisted on purchasing some years earlier, although Sarah had told him it wasn't necessary since the plot of her family, the Baums, would be available. "I've spent my life listening to your relatives," he said. "I'm not going to spend eternity listening to them as well."

Sarah Epstein

Now a widow, Sarah continued to lead a full, useful life surrounded by children, grandchildren, her brothers and her many friends. She was still speaking at public meetings while in her seventies. But now she took time off for vacation trips to Mexico, the West Coast, Hawaii and elsewhere, traveling alone and, wherever possible, by bus. Her children felt that she would be safer and more comfortable traveling by railroad and booked her a trip to California in a Pullman car. Sarah waved goodbye to the family as the train pulled out of Pennsylvania Station, but at Pittsburgh she disembarked and continued the rest of the trip by Greyhound bus. She explained later that the train was too dull and impersonal, whereas whenever she was on a bus she found herself in the company of a group of people who soon became her friends.

In her last years she lived alone in an apartment at The Bolivar on Central Park West, where she was visited by a steady stream of family members and figures prominent in New York City public life. She now attended the S.A.J. Synagogue, where she never missed a Sabbath service unless she was ill, and where she sang in the choir until she was eighty. "Her deep alto voice," her family recalled, "would loudly resound throughout the house of worship. Sometimes while the choir was still performing, she would nod her head and doze off; but a minute or two later she would wake up suddenly, immediately catch up with the choir and continue singing."

Her birthday, which fell on St. Patrick's Day, was now and then the occasion for a gala family reunion and dinner attended by Baums, Websters, Crohns, Epsteins,

Ruskays and the rest, many coming from the South or Midwest, and where the festivities lasted well past midnight. On her seventy-fifth birthday, the New York Chapter of Hadassah did a "This is Your Life" in her honor at the Hotel Astor, at which George Schuster, President of Hunter College, Mordecai Kaplan of the Jewish Theological Seminary and other notables spoke. When one lady guest said, "Mrs. Epstein, I hope I shall live long enough to attend your eightieth birthday party," Sarah replied, "I hope you do, too."

She died at the age of eighty-five. The "Sarah Epstein Group of Hadassah" in New York and the Children's Corner of the library at a Youth Aliyah village in Palestine memorialize her name.

Judith

The Epstein children grew up in a household where the Zionist movement was constantly being discussed. Calling for the establishment in Palestine of a national home for displaced and suppressed Jews, especially those in Eastern Europe, the movement was born in 1897 at the First Zionist Congress in Basle, Switzerland, called by Theodore Herzl, a young Viennese journalist. It had already attracted a small but growing core of enthusiastic adherents among New York's Jewish intelligentsia, including Eddie and Sarah Epstein. Even while still in high school Judith was collecting small contributions for the purchase of land in Palestine in the familiar blue-and-white box with the Star of David on the outside. A few years later, after graduating from Hunter College and while teaching English at Julia Richmond High School, she joined Hadassah. She met her future husband Moses P. Epstein (no relation) at a Hadassah fund-raising party.

After they were married, the young couple moved to Far Rockaway, Long Island, where during the latter days of World War I, Judith, now a young mother, was a familiar sight in the community, wheeling a baby carriage which contained in addition to her infant son, a supply of Hadassah and Zionist pamphlets which she handed out to all and sundry. When the family moved back to Manhattan, Judith became president of he growing West End Hadassah chapter. It marked the beginning of a career with that organization that lasted over seventy years, during which she served as its national president four times; a career which paralleled the fateful events in the Holy Land from the Balfour Declaration of 1917, promising a Jewish homeland in Palestine, to the birth of the State of Israel and beyond, including the three Arab-Jewish wars that followed, events in which Judith was destined to play a prominent role.

The voluminous archives at Hadassah's national headquarters in New York City are a treasure trove of official documents, minutes of meetings, copies of speeches, correspondence and other material reflecting its activities from the first decade of the century to date, including several large boxes containing the papers of Judith Epstein. Even a cursory examination of this huge amount of material, and the analysis, almost at random, of a small fraction of the Epstein papers conveys a picture of an extraordinary career.

Hadassah Accomplishments

The goal of Hadassah was, as Judith described it in a convention address, nothing less than

> "to bring modern American standards of preventative medicine, public health, child welfare and vocational education to the Palestine of 1912, then part of the Ottoman Empire, untouched by the currents of the twentieth century, with a population a large percentage of which believed in witchcraft and ancient tribal remedies, utterly lacking in good hospitals, adequate sanitation and a national health program."

In March 1933 Judith, as national secretary, was called upon to go to Palestine to make a survey of Hadassah's medical and health facilities. It was the first of twenty-five such trips that she would make in her lifetime, and she took her mother Sarah and her two children with her. Her non-stop schedule involved meetings and conferences with Zionist leaders, establishing new hospitals and medical clinics in Tiberius and elsewhere in the country, hiring of additional nurses and other personnel, supervising budgetary and expense problems, and dealing with a host of other details down to providing for the washing of dirty linen at the Rothschild Hospital complex in Jerusalem. Busy as she was, she never lost her enthusiasm for the country, writing to her colleagues in New York:

> "The trips outside of Tel Aviv have been a continuous voyage of discovery. The country is beautiful, the drive to Jerusalem a magnificent experience. I fell in love with Jerusalem at first sight. I imagine one never tires of it, the picturesque Old City, the hills, the walls, and the clear, bracing air."

By 1939 Hadassah's mission in Palestine had been to a large extent accomplished. It had built the Rothschild Hadassah University Hospital and Medical Center in Jerusalem on Mount Scopus, along with an associated X-Ray Diagnostic and Therapy Institute, a Pathological and Radiology Institute and a Neurosurgical Department–all of them operating according to American standards of hospital administration and efficiency, and available to all, Arabs, Christians and Jews, without discrimination. In addition it supported a Home Medical Service for needy patients, a Convalescent Day Care Home, a separate tuberculosis hospital, modern facilities furnishing pre-natal care for mothers and child care for children and adolescents, a School Hygiene Department, occupational therapy and rehabilitation units for the sick and disabled and nurses training schools throughout the country.

In a radio speech on the 25th anniversary of its founding, Judith recalled Hadassah's initial tentative experiment in 1913 under the guidance of its founder Henrietta Szold, when it sent two young American nurses to attempt to alleviate the health problems of the Palestine population.

"The year 1913 might have been the Middle Ages," she said, "so untouched had been the little land in the Near East, the Holy Land, the shrine of pilgrims, the cradle of the three great religions of the world. Picturesque, romantic and colorful it was, but accompanying this picturesqueness was the poverty, superstition and ignorance of the people who lived there–ignorance of those modern discoveries of science which have made the life and lot of mankind so much happier and richer. There was general skepticism and prophesies of inevitable failure for those two intrepid young Americans, but with a sense of romance and that pioneering spirit through which frontiers have been pushed back and civilization has been carried onward, they went undaunted to undertake their difficult tasks–good health ambassadors from the New World to the Old."

Hadassah Enters the Political Arena

In August 1937 Judith led the first Hadassah delegation to the World Zionist Congress in Zurich attended by all the leading Zionist figures, including Chaim Weitzman, David Ben Gurion, Dr. Judah Magnes and Lord Melchett. Up to this time Hadassah had been treated by the Zionist leadership with almost condescension. Even now, the young women delegates were referred to by some, sub rosa, as "school girls" because of their supposed political naiveté. The big issue was whether to negotiate with the British, who governed the country under the mandate of the League of Nations, and with the Arabs, a British proposal for partition of Palestine into two states, one Arab and the other Jewish; or whether to adhere to the hitherto fundamental Zionist principle of an undivided country as a national homeland for the Jewish people. The Hadassah women, maintaining that Arabs and Jews could live peaceably side by side in an undivided country, voted with the majority against partition.

A few months later early in 1938, Judith, having been recently elected national president, reemphasized that Hadassah, in addition to its health and medical activities would from now on inject itself into the political arena.

The Looming Crisis for the Jews of Europe

It now seems incredible that until the late 1930s most Americans and even most of its political establishment were not fully aware of the frightful implications of the ascension to power of Hitler's National Socialist Party in Germany, although for several years the Zionists and Hadassah had been warning of the perilous situation of German and East European jewry. Indeed, up to this time most American Jews had been indifferent, and even opposed, to the concept of Zionism and the creation of a Jewish homeland.

On July 14, 1938 Mrs. Epstein was on the air on a national radio hook-up exhorting American Jews and non-Jews to contribute funds to the Youth Aliyah movement of which Hadassah was the U.S. representative, which was frantically engaged in trying to rescue European Jewish children and bringing them to Israel.

> "In the safe haven of Palestine," she said, "we have the first ray of light in a bleak picture. In 1914 there were about 50,000 Jews in Palestine under Turkish rule. Today under the British mandatory power there is a strong, well-rooted proud community of 475,000 souls, men and women who have given everything they have to the land and their people. . . "

In 1939, on the even of World War II, Judith again led the Hadassah delegation to the World Zionist Organization meeting in Geneva. The crisis had deepened. The British government had issued its infamous "White Paper" barring further Jewish immigration to Palestine. At the Congress Ben Gurion

Judith Epstein

declared "We will fight the White Paper as if there were no war, and we will fight the war as if there were no White Paper!" The German tanks were already rolling into Poland when the meeting was adjourned, and Judith and the other American delegates barely managed to squeeze on board the S.S. Queen Mary before it sailed on its last voyage as a civilian vessel.

The World War II Years

The war years were frightening and frustrating for Hadassah and the Zionists in the United States. Jewish men and women in Palestine flocked in large numbers to form their own regiments in support of British and other allied troops in Syria and elsewhere in the Near East, some even volunteering to fight in Europe; and Hadassah contributed its formidable medical facilities–hospitals, clinics, doctors and nurses–for the allied cause and played an active role in selling U.S. War Bonds in the United States. But Zionist and Hadassah leaders were frantic at their inability to rescue their imperiled co-religionists in Europe; and as news started to emerge of concentration camps and mass slaughter in gas chambers, they launched a major effort to persuade the U.S. government to assist in the rescue attempt.

In November 1942, Judith told Hadassah's Executive Committee that its primary task was to mobilize American public opinion in the United States,

"the land that is playing a stellar role in this war and that will inevitably have a deciding voice in the establishment of world peace and a better international order . . . Our Zionist political objectives are in consonance with the ideals set forth in the Atlantic Charter . . . If the bloodshed and the destruction of the war are not to be in vain, then the crushed and oppressed must be given a new chance for life; and among them the Jewish people returning to its age-old land, sending its roots into the soil reclaiming the wastes, and making of them a flourishing garden for the generations to come."

President Roosevelt was approached. Typically, he accorded the delegation led by Rabbi Stephen Wise a warm welcome and promised to take the matter of rescuing the Jews of Europe up with the British and French governments. But Roosevelt's actions, as was so often the case, didn't match his words, and nothing was done. But Eleanor Roosevelt, the President's wife, was another story. Years before in 1934 she had accepted the invitation to address a Hadassah convention at which Judith had presided as chairwoman, and had gone out of her way to pay tribute to Hadassah's accomplishments in Palestine, which she later was to see with her own eyes on a trip to the Holy Land. Now she agreed to accept the national chairmanship of the Youth Aliyah and added her voice to the rescue efforts in an appeal to people of all faiths throughout the world. Years later when asked to review the events of this terrifying period, Judith described Mrs. Roosevelt as "a towering figure, perhaps the finest human being of her generation."

Incidentally, the Hadassah archives, so rich in all kinds of interesting bits of memorabilia, contain the following letter to Mrs., Epstein from Mrs. Roosevelt, which, apart from indicating how extraordinarily busy Judith must have been, serves to remind us that the First Lady led the life of an independent career woman, with her own menage in New York City, decades before the Women's Liberation Movement of recent years.

"29 Washington Square West
Apartment 15 A
New York, N.Y. 11

Dear Mrs. Epstein:

I have arranged a meeting of the heads of leading women's organizations to discuss grassroots education methods with respect to the United Nations, to take place on September 10th at 10 A.M. at my apartment at 29 Washington Square West. I would be so pleased if you were to attend on behalf of Hadassah.

Yours Sincerely,

Eleanor Roosevelt

In February 1944 Judith appeared before the House Foreign Relations Committee in Washington and testified at great length about the work of Hadassah in Palestine. At the hearing Congressman Eaton asked her:

"Would the witness tell the Committee the meaning of the word 'Hadassah'?"
"It is the Hebrew word for Esther," Mrs. Epstein replied.

Mr. Eaton then gallantly responded: "Esther was a queen, and it appears she has some gifted descendants."

The Critical Post-War Years

In 1946, although the war in Europe was over, the predicament of the Jewish refugees was more desperate then ever. Great Britain as the mandatory power in Palestine, in an effort to win the favor of the Grand Mufti of Jerusalem and of Arab rulers in the Mideast because of their control of the world's largest oil resources, was turning back thousands of concentration camp survivors who sought to enter the country.

In the meantime bloody fighting between Arabs and Jews had already broken out, with Jewish leaders claiming that the British were closing their eyes to the build-up of Arab forces while they declared the organization of Jewish defense fighters illegal. After an extraordinary meeting of the American Zionist Council, Judith, in a radio address, called on Americans

"not to be taken in by British propaganda designed to secure advance sympathy for its illegal acts against the Jewish people . . . the Socialist government under Prime Minister Ernest Bevin is appeasing the Arabs by openly permitting their leaders to build up their troops in the Holy Land . . . at a time when the defense forces of the Jewish people are being hounded and provoked, and boatloads of desperate Jews seeking refuge are being brutally turned back in defiance of the Balfour Declaration and the Anglo-American Committee's recommendation that 100,000 Jews be permitted to enter Palestine immediately."

At the same time, while unsparing in her criticism of the British and her praise of the Hagannah, the Jewish resistance fighters, Judith and most other Jewish leaders deplored and disavowed the activities of Jewish terrorists and extremist groups, the Irgun and the Stern Gang, which were responsible for the bombing of British Headquarters in the King David Hotel and of the Goldsmith British Officer's Club in Jerusalem, actions which only served to give the British authorities a pretext to search Jewish settlements for arms and an excuse to impose martial law.

On July 24, 1947, two hours before she boarded a plane for Palestine to supervise expansion of medical facilities for the newly arriving refugees from Europe, Mrs. Epstein addressed a large outdoor mass meeting in Madison Square Garden in New York to protest the refusal of the British to permit 4500 Jewish concentration camp survivors on the S.S. Exodus to land in the Holy Land.

> "When I arrive," she said, "I shall tell the Jews of Palestine of the outpouring of American indignation and horror at these latest acts of violence. Americans of all races and creeds are showing here today that we will not remain unmoved while men and women who have a legal right to enter their homeland are beaten, shot at, and violently thrust back into the chaotic prison camp that is Europe for them today."

The next day she was traveling by armored car from the Lydda Airport to Tel Aviv. She toured Palestine from border to border in spite of military controls, with rocket and small arms fire going on around her, visiting Jewish army groups and agricultural settlements besieged by Arab snipers and artillery, while at the same time a bitter civil war was raging against British rule.

On November 29, 1947 the United Nations General Assembly, over the bitter opposition of all of the Arab members, approved a Security Council recommendation for the partition of Palestine and the creation of separate Arab and Jewish states; and shortly thereafter, the resolution was endorsed by the U.S. Senate and House of Representatives.

Although the well-meaning Warren Austin, the chief U.S. delegate to the United Nations, unaware of the irony in his phraseology, pleaded, "for the Arabs and Jews to sit down together and settle this matter of Partition in the true Christian spirit," the Arab delegates unanimously rejected the proposal. But the World Zionist Organization, now deeply concerned about British intransigence and Arab violence, and uneasy about powerful anti-Zionist influences in the United States, reversed its long-standing demand for a single Palestinian State, and after an agonizing debate, accepted the concept of partition. Weeks later, with Arabs attacking Jewish settlements and creating havoc in the cities all over Palestine, and with the British forces doing nothing to protect its Jewish inhabitants, Judith went on the air again in the United States:

"The defiance of the Arab States," she said, "which echoed through the halls at Flushing Meadows has taken concrete form. Syria and Lebanon have been used as staging areas for the attacks of the so-called volunteers supplied with arms and uniforms by states that are members of the United Nations and parties to the decision of that international body. Meanwhile the mandatory power, Great Britain, that declines to enforce partition but stated that it would enforce law and order, has refused to use its strong military machine of men and materials to crush outbreaks that not only threaten law and order, but desecrate every principle of international law and decency. And the United States government that played such an important part in bringing about the decision, acts toward Jew and Arab alike, negating that decision by its refusal to sell arms to either of the contestants. Is there no difference between aggressor and victim?"

In the spring of 1948, after the U.S. State Department reversed itself and failed to support the implementation of the United Nations' decision to establish a Jewish state in Palestine, and instead proposed some sort of trusteeship for the country, Judith termed the action "One of the blackest stains on our national honor," and a "brutal assault upon the United Nations."

Jewish Statehood

On May 14, 1948 the temporary Jewish government issued its Proclamation of the State of Israel. But the Arabs rejected all proposals for a truce, and although President Truman announced the United States recognition of the new state, the bitter Arab-Jewish war went on. In July Judith, as Chairman of Hadassah's National Political Committee, and the American Zionist Emergency Council called on the U.N. Security Council to impose sanctions against the Arabs under its U.N. Charter and President Truman and Secretary of State Marshall not only to instruct the United States U.N. delegation to support sanctions, but to modify the American Middle East Arms Embargo so that Israel could obtain weapons for its defense.

Eventually, after a truce was agreed to and hostilities had ended, Judith in an address to Zionist leaders as to future goals, philosophized about the futility of war.

"What a tragic waste war is," she said. "We have lost not only thousands of brave young people but the future leadership that might have made outstanding contributions to the life of the land and its people. Men were immobilized, crouched behind their rifles and machine guns who were thirsting to go out into the fields to fructify them, to build cities and to make the land a great shining example, not only for the Jews who are coming into it from all corners of the world, but for the Middle East of which it is a part . . ."

The Post-War Years

Judith was National President of Hadassah from 1937 to 1939, and from 1943 to 1947. Thereafter, she served as Chairman of its Political Action Committee and on other important committees for the rest of her life, continuing her dizzy pace, never letting up. Her colleague Fannie Cohen insists that many of Hadassah's nearly 400,000 present members, stirred by Judith's ardor and enthusiasm, joined after hearing her address a meeting. She was constantly in demand as a speaker. In March of 1949, while she was touring the West Coast addressing meetings one after another in Seattle, San Francisco and Los Angeles, Mrs. Tamar de Sola Pool wrote her from New York headquarters:

"I shall never cease to marvel at your ability to write letters in the non-existent interims of your busy schedule. The Boston Chapter was deeply disappointed that you could not address its gala meeting this week. We wish that in addition to all your other gifts, you had the one of being able to be in two places at the same time."

Asked once how she became such a good public speaker, Judith replied:

"When I and my two brothers were children, my mother Sarah insisted that at the supper table every night each of us would have to relate in detail to her and my father what we had done during the day. 'Say what you like,' she said. 'but make it interesting.' It seems to have been excellent training."

Judith on the platform was indeed outstanding–lucid, forceful and able to stir the emotions of her audience with her sincerity, and to charm them with her wit and grace. At the same time she displayed an excellent knowledge of history and contemporary world problems. Incredible as it may seem, she never wrote out or dictated her speeches in advance, but spoke extemporaneously, with at most a few notes on a slip of paper.

She was sometimes compared to another great orator, her friend Abba Eban, Israel's chief representative at the United Nations. However they were quite different. Neither Judith, nor anyone else for that matter, could emulate the scintillating eloquence, the scholarly phraseology and witty asides of Mr. Eban. On the other hand, he was not capable, as was Judith, of bringing an audience to its feet in a thunder of applause.

In a speech in Detroit in 1952 she explained how difficult some problems were to solve with a colorful analogy.

"Nothing in Israel is simple. Men often say to me: 'After all, you people in Hadassah ought to understand that when you build a house, it is important that it must first have a foundation. After that you build the first story, and then the

179

second story can be built.' But it is not that simple. In Israel they are laying the foundation at the same time that they are working on the roof, which is inevitable if one is to introduce the twentieth century at a rapid tempo into a medieval land."

On another occasion she pondered the impact of modern Israel on the native population:

"I was recently at the Israel border in Huleh," she said, "where Israeli workers were using a huge machine to dredge the bed of the river to widen and deepen it. I looked across the tiny bridge, half of which is in Israel, half in Syria, and saw a group of curious Syrians who were looking on. I tried to imagine what was in their minds. The machine looked like a huge monster. One man sat at the controls, and, as he touched the lever, the river bed gave up its water, mud and dirt, performing with one movement an operation that would require many, many man hours of manual labor. At another spot, what was once a swampland was being drained and turned into hundreds of acres of land for the cultivation of fruits and vegetables to feed the people of the country. Could these Syrians escape the connection between the machine and the fact that they will eat better because of it? Would they begin to understand that perhaps there is something in Western Civilization beyond cannons, tanks and guns? May they not be beginning to equate the West with machinery that brings forth food out of the earth?"

The Impact of One Woman

As one leafs through the thousands of papers and documents in the Hadassah archives, one cannot help but sense the impact that Mrs. Epstein had on the dramatic events in the Mideast during the critical years about a half century ago. No one can doubt that because of American prestige and influence, recognition of Israel's statehood depended largely on the attitude of the United States government. The effect of Judith's voice, day after day, week after week, here and abroad, addressing audiences in auditoriums or on national radio broadcasts, and her words in press releases and magazine articles as a molder of opinion was enormous. But beyond that, she was able to enlist, as additional advocates, the voices of some 150,000 members of Hadassah's 600 chapters around the country, each of them eager to spread the word in her own community. The result was overwhelming public support in this country, which in turn prompted President Truman's decisive action.

Is it too much to suggest that it was the activity of this woman, perhaps more than that of any other individual in this country, which led to the creation of the Jewish state?

Moses P. Epstein and the Family Home

The Baum-Webster Bugle, the "newspaper" specially printed for the occasion of a Baum-Webster clan family reunion at a New York City hotel on November 28, 1953, contained a number of thumb-nail verses kidding various members of the family, including this one about Judith's husband, Moses P. Epstein, whom no one called anything but "Moe."

"My name's in the phonebook,
For all folks to see

But the calls are for Judith
Damned few are for me."

In spite of the implication that Moe was a very second fiddle in the Epstein household, he was in fact an impressive person in his own right. A vice-president of the Industrial Rayon Corporation, he was a leading figure in the clothing industry, with a scholar's knowledge of business and economics. Beyond that, as a veteran Zionist, he was very much involved in his wife's political activities. Judith often said that she discussed everything she did with him and indeed never made an important decision without consulting him beforehand. He also had a dry sense of humor that was revealed when he was called upon to speak at family gatherings.

The Epstein dinner parties were famous, although it was Moe, something of a gourmet chef, who did the cooking. As for Judith, cooking was not on her list of priorities. Her friend Fanny Cohen, when asked about Judith's cooking, said: "Judith's cooking? She didn't know how to boil water!"

When David, Judith's son, was released at the end of the war after being taken prisoner by the Germans, he and his companions were interviewed by the press, and each was asked the ritualistic question of what he most looked forward to when he got home. One said, "My mom's home-baked apple pies." Another, "My wife's chocolate layer cake," and so forth. David's reply was "Those marvelous pastries my mother buys at the Viennese bake shop on 86th Street."

New Year's Day was open house at Judith and Moe's. Everybody who was anybody in Jewish affairs dropped by. The first time Michael Comay, Israel's Ambassador to the U.N., was in New York, he asked his colleagues what they were doing on New Year's Day. Everyone replied, "We're going to the Epsteins, of course. "I didn't know," he said, "who the Epsteins were, but I found their address and showed up at the door." It was the beginning of a long friendship.

The Epsteins didn't have much time to spend with their children–they were too busy. When they had a free night, they often went downtown to the Roseland Ballroom to dance. They were both excellent dancers.

A Very Modest Person

Despite her prominence and the adulation showered on her, Judith was always gracious and extremely modest. One day when her daughter asked what should be done with an accumulation of papers and correspondence in a closet at home, she told her to throw it all out; and she was astonished when told that two young Hadassah members were preparing her biography. Each time that she was re-elected president of the organization, she received congratulatory letters from all over the world. Her response to one such letter from Moshe Sharett, Israel's Prime Minister, was typical:

"I have been personally enriched," she wrote, "by the affectionate regard which I have been fortunate to receive from all of you. I only wish I felt equal to the enormous responsibilities which face us all."

Once at an international conference in Geneva, she fell into a conversation with an Italian diplomat who asked her, "But Mrs. Epstein, you don't speak French, or Spanish or Italian?" "No," she replied, I speak only English, but I speak it very well." Modest though she was, she knew her own worth.

Shortcomings? Could someone like Judith have had shortcomings? When her colleagues celebrated her birthday one year with an affectionate "roasting," they were hard put to it to find foibles to make fun of, apart from her indifference to her dress and appearance in her early days. She rarely bothered to have her hair done, her dress never matched her scarf, and her stockings didn't match her shoes. When she mounted the dais, more often than not her slip would be showing.

The Last Years

Over the course of her career, Judith had gotten to know all the leading personalities active in Jewish affairs both in the United States and abroad, including of course various Prime Ministers and other important officials in Israel–David Ben Gurion, Golda Meier, Chaim Weizman, Levi Eshkol, Abba Eban, Moshe Sharett, Stephen S. Wise, Louis Brandeis, Abbe Hillel Silver, Teddy Kollek and the rest. Shortly before his death she went to see Dr. Weizman, the long-time President of the World Zionist Congress and Israel's first President, in Rohoboth in Israel, when he was already nearly blind. He said to her, "Judith dear, come to the window. Perhaps in the bright light I can see you." When he realized that he could not, he caressed the outline of her face with his hands, kissed her and said, "Judith you're still special."

During the 1980s, although she was now revered by Hadassah as a sort of elder stateswoman, Judith felt for the first time alienated from a large segment of its membership due to disagreement over the question of how best to achieve peace between Israel and the Palestinians, the same issue that was dividing the rest of the American Jewish community. Judith was a "dove" who favored surrendering "land for peace," the giving up of part of the West Bank and the Gaza Strip if necessary. This resulted in frequent and sometimes acrimonious arguments with her colleagues in Hadassah.

Nevertheless Judith continued to be active in the organization until she was almost ninety, serving on important committees, and even occasionally addressing Hadassah meetings around the country.

She died in 1988 at the age of 92. A speaker who followed her on the platform at a large Hadassah convention when Judith was in her mid-eighties remarked:

> "Magic took hold of the audience as this petite, white-haired woman, grown old in the service of her people, approached the dais. The delegates stood and with tremendous sustained applause, welcomed her. She was a hard act to follow.

Josh

When Josh (Joshua), Eddie and Sarah Epstein's older son, was graduated from City College, he sought his father's advice as to what he should do. "Take any job," his strictly religious father told him, "so long as you don't have to work on shabbas" (Saturday). Josh found employment with a large ladies dress manufacturer. This was a mistake. His parents should have encouraged him to go to graduate school and become a teacher. A born pedagogue, Josh would have made an admirable college professor.

After a while he quit the dress business to go into advertising, for which, with his keen inventive mind and understanding of business practices, he was well qualified. Unable to land a job with any of the leading advertising agencies, he started his own small agency, later taking in his younger brother Abbe as a partner. But large, well-paying accounts were hard to come by and after a few years Josh was obliged to go out of business.

By a stroke of good fortune, just as he was dissolving his own agency, another new small advertising agency was being formed by three bright young men. One of them, Maxwell Dane, was a friend of Josh, and invited him to join their new firm, Doyle, Dane and Bernbach, which after a few years became one of the most innovative and successful agencies in the city. Josh brought to the new firm one important account that he had managed to acquire for his own agency, the Kosher Foods Division of the H.J. Heinz Company, the canned food products giant. A few years earlier Josh had convinced the Heinz company management that there was a huge, untapped market for their soups and other foods if they were to make a special line of kosher products, which Josh's agency would reach via advertisements in Jewish and Yiddish newspapers and magazines. Josh remained a partner in Doyle, Dane and Bernbach for many years, and when he left to again operate his own agency, he took the Heinz account with him and continued to handle it with great success for the rest of his business career.

He married Elizabeth, a former school teacher, a charming, well-educated woman who shared his intellectual and cultural tastes. They moved first to Sunnyside and later to Woodmere, Long Island, where they brought up their two children and became active in community affairs. Both had good voices and like to sing, and they found an outlet for their love of music as members of the United Choral Society directed by David Randolph, which gave a series of concerts in the Rockaway area.

However the pedagogue and crusader in Josh was bound to surface. He had always been clever writing skits and humorous poetry for family parties. But deep down he was a very serious, socially-conscious individual. As he grew older he became increasingly critical of what he saw as the awesome problems that were plaguing the country–the extremes of wealth and poverty, crime, fascism and the rest–and more and more skeptical of the ability of our capitalist society to deal with them.

During the 1930s and 1940s, with the rise of Hitler, the crushing of democracy in Czechoslovakia, and the feeble and ineffectual attempts of the French and British governments at appeasement, Josh, like so many other progressives in this country, became radicalized. He saw in the Soviet Union the only power prepared to confront the menace of fascism. Although he never became a member of the Communist Party, by the beginning of

World War II, Josh was a fervent admirer and defender of the Soviet Union. Even the stories of Stalin's crimes, which would later be confirmed as true, of mass deportations of peasants to Siberia, of the staged trials of generals and dissidents, not even the Nazi-Soviet Pact for the partition of Poland caused his faith in the Soviet Union to waiver.

It was thus almost predictable when a group of political activists on the South Shore of Long Island formed the Five Towns Community Forum, that Josh, a fine speaker, would be one of its founders, and later its chairman.

One of the thorniest and most controversial of the social and political subjects discussed and debated at the Forum was that of Israel, an especially touchy one in a community with a large Jewish population, most of them now ardent Zionists. Josh and a number of others adhered to a rigidly anti-zionist point of view which also happened to be the Communist Party position, that Israel was an imperialist state, a pawn for United States ambitions in the Near East, and an oppressor of its Arab population.

Needless to say this infuriated his sister Judith, the four times President of Hadassah and a prominent Zionist. They had always loved and admired one another. But now, as the result of Josh's vehement anti-Israel attitude, he and Judith rarely spoke to one another; and when they occasionally met at family gatherings, the subject was carefully avoided.

Even after the revelations by Khrushchev of the crimes and deceptions of the Stalin era, when even formerly die-hard Communists left the Party, Josh refused to be swayed. He passed away, however, before the complete unraveling of the Soviet mystique in the late 1980s.

When Josh's wife Elizabeth died, Josh was inconsolable and for a while retreated into isolation. But gradually he resumed his participation in community affairs and one night, at a Five Towns Forum meeting where he was the principle speaker, he met and shortly thereafter married Fanny, a splendid woman who proved to be a most affectionate and compatible companion and stepmother of his two children.

His son David, an outstanding musician, head of the Department of Music at M.I.T., perhaps supplied the most rational explanation of his father's stubborn refusal to abandon his "Communistic" views. Josh, he said, was more a relentless critic of American capitalism than a worshiper of the Soviet Union. A firm believer in an ideal socialist society that he felt ultimately would emerge in Russia, he refused to change. "In the last analysis," his son observed, "Josh was like his father Eddie, a man of great honesty and integrity, who stubbornly adhered to the views he believed in."

Abbe, My Favorite Cousin

Youth

A family story has it that one day, when Sarah Epstein's younger son Abbe was still in high school, Dr. Mordecai Kaplan, the celebrated professor of the Jewish Theological Seminary and a close friend of the family, dropped in for a visit. Entering the apartment he noticed Abbe's report card lying on the table in the foyer, examined it and saw the notation: "Reproved again this month for repeatedly talking during class!" "So he's a talker too!" Dr. Kaplan said to Sarah. Every one of the Epsteins–Sarah, Judith, Josh and Abbe–were "talkers." In any group of people engaged in a discussion, they soon dominated the conversation. It was as if, obliged to listen to voices expressing a variety of opinions, they preferred hearing their own.

Abbe was an adventurous young man. After high school, at eighteen, he and a friend decided to tour Europe. They managed to work their way across the Atlantic with jobs as busboys on a Cunard steamship and had a fine time in Paris and London. But having spent all their money, returning home was a problem. Lacking funds for passage, they stowed away on the S.S. George Washington, were soon discovered, put in the ship's prison and released only to swab the decks and do other menial jobs. Fortunately they met a passenger who knew Abbe's family and who sent them a cablegram. When the ship docked in New York, Abbe's father was waiting, posted a bond and they were released.

Abbe went to Columbia College, where he played on the tennis team, and then attended its School of Journalism. After serving briefly in the Coast Guard, he got a job as a reporter with the Paris *Herald Tribune* and went off to live in France. He was bright, personable, had a great sense of humor and was physically very attractive, although not handsome in the conventional sense. Everyone predicted a brilliant future for him.

Abbe and Judith Sheinberg

During all this time, apart from seeing him once or twice at large family gatherings, I didn't know Abbe at all. However, by a curious coincidence, I did get to know the young woman who later was to become his first wife. Our family, the Ruskays, lived for years on New McNeil Avenue in Lawrence, Long Island; and at one period when I was fourteen or fifteen, a family by the name of Sheinberg, with two sons and an older daughter, Judith, became our next-door neighbors. Young as I was, Judith made a powerful impression on me. With jet black hair, dark eyes, a slightly aquiline nose, sultry features and a lovely figure, she was exceptionally beautiful and very popular. When she went out, there were always two or three young men, not just one, who would call for her. She seemed to be part of a somewhat exclusive, almost elite set of young people, more fashionable and sophisticated than others in the community. Then one day, quite abruptly, the family left New McNeil Avenue and moved back to Manhattan, when Mr. Sheinberg's business went into bankruptcy. A year or two later, out of the blue, we heard that Judith was married, and, of all people, to my cousin Abbe. The wedding, a niece of Abbe recalls, was a splendid affair. The couple sailed for Europe on their wedding trip with first-class accommodations and made for Paris, where Abbe resumed his reporter's job with the *Herald Tribune*.

But apparently things didn't go so well for Abbe in Paris. The late 1920s were exhilarating times for journalists in Europe. William Shirer, John Gunther and other reporters on the *Herald Tribune* were making names for themselves and were being rapidly promoted. But somehow, although Abbe wrote some excellent pieces, they seemed never to catch the eye of the editor. He continued to be mired in the same routine assignments, and his salary remained the same.

At the same time his married life started to unravel. Always fascinated by good-looking women, Abbe had married impulsively, carried away by Judith's beauty, imagining that she shared his ideals, and his interest in literature, politics and other people. But now with their constant lack of money and need to economize, her true character was revealed as spoiled, selfish, shallow and materialistic. One day in 1929 Abbe returned to their little apartment in the Left Bank and found that she had left him. With their marriage broken up, Abbe returned to New York, broke, hurt and completely discouraged.

As for Judith, after the divorce she remarried. Her new husband, a fine decent man and well-to-do, the owner of a large chain of trade magazines, accepted her for what she was. Now she had what she had always wanted, a wealthy husband, a Park Avenue apartment, and a house in the suburbs, not to mention a vacation home in Arizona. She had no real interests but remained for the rest of her life a dilettante–vain, self-centered, satisfied so long as she attracted men and was the center of attention. However, later in life she lost her good looks and became bitter and withdrawn.

A Checkered Career

Abbe now gave up journalism, and hoping to capitalize on his imagination and writing skills, sought to make a living in advertising, publicity and sales promotion. For a while his brother Josh took him in as a partner in his advertising agency. After that he drifted from one job or project to another, managing to make a living, not much more. Success always seemed to elude him. His bad luck was incredible. Foreseeing the need for a long-lasting men's razor blade, he managed to secure for himself the exclusive rights for the sale and distribution in the United States of the Personna Blade, made in Sweden and already successful in Europe. He spent weeks on its promotion here, managing to persuade Brooks Brothers, Saks Fifth Avenue, Dunhill and other high quality shops to feature it in a month-long sales test period. The results were disappointing and he gave up, surrendering the distributorship. A year later someone else who had taken over the distribution rights tried again, this time with a larger group of retailers and for a longer test period, and the campaign succeeded, slowly at first. But thereafter sales accelerated rapidly, and eventually made a fortune for the new entrepreneur.

It was at this point in his life, in the mid-1930s, that I got to know Abbe. Although he was six or seven years older than I, we were both bachelors. To me he was everything admirable—educated, charming, witty and fun to be with, in spite of his troubles. In my eyes there were no limits to what he could have achieved. He would have made a perfect diplomat. Some people felt that there was a character failing, a lack of perseverance or aggressiveness. I never believed that. To me it was just a case of persistent bad luck.

Abbe, however, never lost his appeal for women. One summer day we were at Atlantic Beach on Long Island, sunning ourselves after a swim. A short distance away, a young woman was sitting by herself under a beach umbrella quietly reading. Abbe suddenly rose to his feet, walked over to her, said something and laughed, and without a word sat down. Obviously surprised, she put down her book and looked at him. He continued to chatter away, completely at ease, as if he were conversing with an old friend. This went on for three or four minutes. Meanwhile she had not said a word. Then Abbe abruptly rose, reached out his hand, and helped her to her feet and they walked toward the surf and went swimming together. He spent that night in her apartment.

Popularity with Women

His success with women was extraordinary. Most of them were bright and intelligent, with careers of some kind, although I recall at least one show girl from Earl Carroll's "Vanities." All of them were good-looking. Abbe invariably brought them to the Hotel Bolivar to meet his mother, Sarah. She received them all graciously, but never stopped hoping that one day her son would find "a nice Jewish girl" and settle down.

He had strong convictions about meeting people who were strangers, deploring the fact that people were prevented from meeting interesting and attractive men and women whom they did not know by the stupid convention which decreed that one did not talk to persons to whom one had not been formally introduced. One day we were walking on Madison Avenue and stopped to examine some paintings in the window of an art boutique. Standing next to us was a young woman who was also examining the window's contents. Suddenly Abbe turned to her and with a little laugh accompanied by his charming smile, said, "I don't know you, and you don't know me, which I think is a great pity because you appear to me a sensitive soul, interested in the same things that interest me." Then with exaggerated seriousness he added, "I find it absurd that I should be deprived of the opportunity of knowing you and that you should be unable to make my acquaintance, simply because of one of society's primitive taboos." By this time the young woman, surprised at first, was laughing, and Abbe introduced himself and me. He had made a new friend.

A week later I was at a Carnegie Hall concert and during the intermission, seeing a pretty young woman sitting alone on the steps of the Dress Circle reading her program, decided to try the same approach. I sat down beside her and made the same little speech, using Abbe's exact words. However the result was not the same. She glared at me in disbelief, got up, hissed the words "You jerk!" over her shoulder and walked away.

A Happy Marriage–Then Tragedy

In the summer of 1939 or 1940, when Abbe and I shared an apartment on West 110th Street, I proved to be a successful matchmaker. We had planned a party for our friends, and, with Abbe in mind, I decided to invite Evelyn, a girl I had known from Woodmere, Long Island, a Wellesley College graduate, very pretty and clever, with a somewhat theatrical British accent that had somehow put me off. When Evelyn arrived at the party I introduced her to Abbe. They literally fell into one another's arms. For the next few weeks they were inseparable, and a month or two later were married. Evelyn evidently found in Abbe everything she saw lacking in me.

From then on he and I lost touch with one another. During World War II I was in the service for three-and-a-half years, most of it overseas, and he was with the Office of War Information, first in London, later in Paris. Early in 1946 I was dispatched by the Signal Corps on a mission to Paris, where I got in touch with Abbe and spent three delightful days with him and his friends. Typically, he seemed to know everyone.

After the war, I was extremely busy for the next few years picking up the threads of my civilian life, resuming my law practice, getting myself married and raising a family on Long Island. Somehow, apart from a single visit to their Greenwich Village apartment, I never saw Abbe or Evelyn again. Years passed and then one day I learned long after the fact that tragedy had struck them not once, but twice, two dreadful, horrible blows.

The Epstein Family (1930)
Top Row: Josh, Abbe, Naomi, Moe and David Epstein
Bottom Row: Elizabeth (Josh's wife), Sarah and Judith Epstein

Both of their children were born mentally and physically retarded and eventually had to be institutionalized.

In spite of everything, they struggled on, trying to make a life for themselves. Then while visiting friends one summer weekend at Candlewood Lake in Connecticut, the final calamity occurred when Abbe, a good athlete, suffered a severe heart attack while swimming offshore. By the time that rescuers got him to the beach, he was dead. He was only forty-seven years old.

Misfortune and tragedy dogged the footsteps of this charming man, my favorite cousin, all of his life. He was, as his niece Naomi Cohen put it, a true F. Scott Fitzgerald character.

CHAPTER VI

THE WEBSTER CLAN – PAUL WEBSTER

The Webster Family Background

Like the Baums, the early forebears of the Webster family, Bernard and Eva Webster, arrived in this country in 1842 from Augustova, a small village in Poland, on the Windjammer "Chester," with their son Jason and their daughter Goldie. It was during the period when all of Central Europe was in the turmoil culminating in the revolution of 1848. Poland was beset with political and religious persecution and was especially inhospitable to Jews, who looked to America as the Promised Land, the land of democracy and opportunity.

With them on the same vessel were their village neighbors David and Eva Baum, their sons Abbe and Israel and their daughters Genesche and Amelia. The two families settled on East Broadway on New York's lower East Side, where virtually all Jewish immigrants lived. Whether or not the young people had been romantically interested in the old country is not known. At any rate the families were soon doubly united by marriage–Abbe marrying Goldie Webster and Jacob marrying Genesche Baum. Subsequently, the family relationship was further enriched when Theodore Crohn married a daughter of Abbe Baum.

How Jacob Webster, whom everyone called "Yank," supported his young wife and growing family in the early years in New York we don't know. Presumably like other recent Jewish immigrants, he made a living as a peddler, or small merchant, or got a job in the growing lower East Side business community. In all likelihood when the Civil War started he and the Baum brothers, as they and other married men with growing children who needed their support were entitled to do, each paid approximately three hundred dollars to a young volunteer to take their place in the army. They witnessed the Draft Riots of 1863 in Central Park and the hanging and slaughtering of innocent negroes in the streets.

According to a family chronicle written by Lawrence Crohn, toward the end or shortly after the Civil War Yank Webster, the Baum brothers and Theodore and Marcus Crohn traveled to western Pennsylvania and opened up a small general store in Titusville, and Yank for a while operated a small shop in nearby Tar Farm.

Eventually Yank returned to New York City and entered the garment business as a manufacturer of women's petticoats. He was a capable, enterprising businessman. As the years went by the business prospered and Yank decided to move his growing family to larger quarters uptown.

The Webster Home

The Webster family of nine children, six boys and three girls, all grew up in a large brownstone private house on Lexington Avenue and 94th Street, not far from Central Park. At the turn of the century upper Fifth Avenue, from 90th Street to 96th Street, was the home of squatters living in wooden shacks who tended sheep and goats. The Webster children remembered being sent there by their mother to buy goat's milk.

The Webster household, Lawrence Crohn recalled "was always filled with good cheer. The entire family was endowed with a sparkling sense of humor so that the walls virtually resounded with gay laughter most of the time. Hospitality was emblazoned on their doormat." Their Baum, Crohn and Ruskay cousins, uncles and aunts were always visiting. My father, Cecil Ruskay, and Burrill Crohn remembered that during their student days at City College they regularly attended the Saturday night poker games at the Websters.

Jacob Webster, "Uncle 'Yank' as we called him," Larry Crohn wrote, "was a social creature. His favorite expression was 'Everybody knows me!' He used to visit us each Saturday after services at the synagogue, where he was a trustee and chief usher. At services he always wore a stove-pipe hat, striped grey trousers, a cut-away coat and grey suede gloves. At our house he would imbibe a big glass of whiskey from a huge demijohn which my father bought for about a dollar. Yank was known as the Petticoat King. In those days women wore several petticoats, one on top of the other. His factory at Duane and Walker Streets turned out satin and messaline petticoats. When petticoats went out of style, he made ladies blouses. He often told us how as a young man he waved goodbye to the 69th Regiment as it left New York City for the Civil War."

Jacob and Lena (Geneshe) Webster

The Colorful Websters

There always seemed to be a party going on at the Webster home. The Festival of Purim was the occasion for a big, boisterous masquerade party. Everyone had to wear a costume with the boys dressing up in dresses and gowns, borrowed from thier mothers and aunts. Every four years the entire clan–Websters, Baums, Crohns and Ruskays and the rest, with their children and grandchildren, sometimes as many as one hundred people–would gather for a large affair at a New York hotel. On these occasions the three Webster "boys," Sidney, Bernie and Leslie, were star performers. Singing and dancing with considerable skill, derby hats on their heads and twirling canes, their renditions of music hall numbers like "On zee bee, on zee boo, en zee boulevard," were greeted with shrieks of laughter. They also conducted a mock-serious ceremony initiating older children and new sons- and daughters-in law into the family, their theme song for this ritual being "hupsy klupsy a la varna, shudery shudery kumin karmi." No one, including themselves, had any idea what these words meant. Sidney, the eldest, was the most amusing. He could circle a ballroom filled with his relatives, old and young, and spontaneously improvise a jingle about each one of them.

Bernie Webster was a cheerful, popular personality and known as a practical joker. He was a cotton salesman, selling spool cotton to the garment trade. Although somewhat hard of hearing, he often pretended to be more deaf than he actually was, writing out orders for double the quantity actually given him. But his customers enjoyed his company so much that they didn't object when they got their bill.

He was also kind and sensitive to the plight of less fortunate persons. At the Webster family synagogue there was a long-standing practice of awarding the coveted honor of leading the prayers from the Book of Jonah on the afternoon of Yom Kippur to one of the rich, influential members of the congregation who bid the most for the distinction. Bernie, far from being a wealthy man, nevertheless decided one year to bid for this prize, and to the astonishment of the congregation won it. But instead of taking it for himself, he called over the sexton and told him to give the honor to a poor but very pious old man sitting in the rear. The well-to-do pillars of the congregation were aghast.

The Long Island Websters

Myron ("Mike") Webster, the eldest of Yank's children, was a very handsome man with white hair and chiseled features. Initially he was a partner with his father in the petticoat business, but later established the wholesale firm of Webster & Aaron Ladies Shirtwaists, and became a director of The Dress Manufacturers' Association. He married Blanche Stonehill, whose family had lived in New York since 1830. Their marriage in Temple Emanuel, then at 42nd Street and Fifth Avenue, of which Blanche's grandfather was one of the founders, was the first wedding to take place there.

Shortly after their marriage the Myron Websters moved to Lawrence, Long Island, buying a charming home which faced a large estate on which sat an old white colonial mansion, an historic landmark known as "Rock Hall," in which General George Washington spent one night during the Battle of Long Island in the Revolutionary War.

Our family, the Ruskays, related to the Websters through my father Cecil, also lived in Lawrence, although in a somewhat less grandiose neighborhood. Unlike the rest of the Websters, the Myron Websters were wealthier, more sedate, almost aristocratic. As Larry Crohn noted, "The Webster chauffeur-driven car was a familiar sight in the area." The Ruskays at that time didn't even own an automobile. While the two families were friendly, they moved in different social circles, although my mother Sophie was able occasionally to recruit Blanche Webster for one of her afternoon play-reading groups. Moreover, the Websters belonged to the Reformed Jewish Temple in Lawrence, while the Ruskays continued to attend the Orthodox Synagogue in Far Rockaway–a significant difference in those days before World War II, when the Reformed Jewish leadership was anti-zionist while we orthodox Jews were fervent Zionists.

Myron had two sons. Morton, the eldest, like his father and mother exceedingly handsome, was with a Wall Street firm which was a member of the New York Stock Exchange, and was considered to be an authority on investment bonds. He dropped out of Cornell after two years during World War I to enlist in the Naval Aviation Service, was sent to the Massachusetts Institute of Technology and emerged an ensign. In World War II he became a Commander in the Navy's Amphibious

Forces and received a citation from the Commander of Southwest Pacific Operations.

Paul Webster, Poet and Adventurer – Beginnings of a Songwriter

Myron Webster's second son was Paul Francis Webster. During the 1920s while a young man, Paul was a frequent visitor in the Ruskay home on Friday nights when my father, Cecil, would give dramatic readings of plays by Shakespeare, Eugene O'Neill or Sean O'Casey, or recite selections from the poetry of Robert Frost or Rombinson Jeffers before an audience of friends and the Ruskay children and their friends. I have a vivid recollection of the young Paul Webster stretched out on the floor of our living room (all of the chairs and the couch were occupied by adults) listening intently. Little did we know that we had a future Academy Award winning lyricist in our midst.

After that, years passed and we lost touch with our young cousin. Meanwhile, Paul attended college at Cornell and New York University, majoring in journalism and philosophy. His father had hoped that he would join him in his highly successful dress manufacturing business, but Paul not only showed no interest in going into the dress business, but also decided against a career in journalism. Instead he chose to lead an adventurous, unconventional life which would at the same time permit him to write poetry and fulfill his dream of becoming a songwriter.

But first he wanted to travel and see the world. In 1927, while still in his twenties, he joined the Merchant Marine and for several years, until 1930, traveled all over the world as an ordinary seaman. It was an exciting, colorful life. Among other dramatic experiences, he served on the S.S. Independence while it was carrying a cargo of high-explosive nitroglycerine to the French Army in Indochina, Another time his ship successfully eluded a blockade by the Chinese Communist troops while delivering a crucial cargo to government forces in Shanghai.

After leaving the Merchant Marine, this ex-sailor, a handsome young man, dapper and always well-dressed, got himself a job at Arthur Murray's Dance Studio in New York City, teaching young women how to do the rumba and tango.

In the early 1930s some of Paul's poetry, which had been published in a school magazine, came to the attention of John Jacob Loeb, a young, extremely talented musician who lived in Woodmere, Long Island, a few miles from the Webster family home in Lawrence. Loeb was eager to find someone to write lyrics for the songs he had been composing.

Curiously enough, I happened to know Johnny Loeb from the days when both of us attended Woodmere Academy as teenagers. He was a big, brawny, jovial, enthusiastic and altogether delightful young man, and a natural genius at the piano, which he taught himself to play. During our high school days Johnny and I would often re-enter the deserted school building after football or baseball practice, steal into the kitchen and raid the ice box for cookies and cake. Then we would go into the music room where John would sit at the piano and play his wonderful arrangements of current popular songs and improvise tunes of his own.

Here was another free, adventurous soul if there ever was one, an ideal counterpart for the talents of Paul Webster.

Several years later I met Johnny at a Woodmere Academy alumni reunion where he was the featured entertainer, and heard him play and sing *Masquerade* and *Two Little Blue Little Eyes*, two hits for which he had written the music to Paul's lyrics. They had found a publisher and undertook to promote their songs themselves. They boldly approached Paul Whiteman, the leader of the best-known band of those days, and persuaded him to record *Masquerade*; and induced Rudee Valee, the famous young crooner, to record *Two Little Blue Little Eyes*, by agreeing to add Vallee's name as co-author.

In the early 1930s Paul and Johnny Loeb led a carefree, rather wild life together, roaming the bars and dives of the Rockaways and the adjacent Five Towns vicinity, drinking and partying in the company of an assortment of girlfriends, meanwhile writing some thirty-three songs together. Then they parted amicably, each deciding to go his separate way.

Johnny had met Guy Lombardo, the popular bandleader, and his brother Carmen and started writing arrangements for their orchestra. He also for a number of years wrote music and arrangements for the legendary Fats Waller and for the summer shows of the Lombardos and other musicians at the Jones Beach outdoor stadium; and his ambitious, elaborate composition, *Reflections in the Water*, was premiered by the great Paul Whiteman band. A big man well over six feet tall, his jovial, good-natured, outgoing personality never changed. His charming wife Janet, a tiny young woman and a talented artist, barely came up to his shoulder. They had two sons, both musicians. At the age of fifty, without any professional instruction, he took up painting and turned out dozens of lovely watercolors. Tragically, he was suddenly stricken with cancer and died prematurely at the age of sixty.

Success on Broadway, On to Hollywood and Marriage

Meanwhile Paul had set his sights on Broadway and then Hollywood. He possessed a unique and prolific talent for writing lyrics that were original, clever, and at the same time full of emotion and subtle meanings. By the mid-1930s he had written the lyrics for a number of top hit songs, including *My Moonlight Madonna* and *Two Cigarettes in the Dark*. He got the idea for the latter song after watching the leading actor and actress in the play *Kill that Story* light each other's cigarettes. He enjoyed the challenge of fitting tunes to odd situations. It wasn't long before he was in demand for writing lyrics for new Broadway shows and revues. When Hollywood started to make musicals during the Depression, he was sought by Twentieth Century Fox and other major studios to write songs for such film stars as Shirley Temple, Bobby Breen and later on for pictures featuring Doris Day, Gene Kelly, Mario Lanza, Pat Boone, Johnny Mathis and others.

At a Hollywood costume party, Paul met and fell in love with Gloria Lenore Benguiat, a beautiful young woman of Spanish ancestry, whose family traced its origins back to the days of Torquemada and the Spanish Inquisition in the 15th century. Gloria's father and uncle were prominent antiquarians. Among the family's possessions were ancient tapestries, one of which now hangs in the Metropolitan Museum of Art in New York City. Another item was the actual throne of Queen Isabella of Spain. Paul and Gloria were married and settled in Beverly Hills, where their home became one of the famous Hollywood showplaces and a frequent gathering spot for actors, actresses, writers and critics and their children.

Throughout the 1940s, 1950s and 1960s, Webster's song hits and theme songs for films followed in rapid order, one after the other. He collaborated with many of the leading composers of the day, including Sammy Fain, Hoagy Carmichael, Duke Ellington, Johnny Green, Andre Previn and Henry Mancini, becoming known as the writer who could compose a lyric for a song that would be appropriate for any film, no matter what the subject. He would sit down with a songwriter right from the inception of they melody's creation, record the song, then go over it time after time, fitting his lyrics gradually to the music. He often worked with a songwriter throughout the night.

Things didn't always come easy. Certain singers like Doris Day and Pat Boone, and some recording companies were reluctant, for one reason or another, to

Paul Webster, George Gershwin and Lou Alter

sing or record a Webster song and did so only after much persuasion. Afterwards they usually found the number to be high on the hit charts. He is best remembered for his many film and title songs, including *Secret Love, Love is a Many Splendored Thing, The Shadow of Your Smile, A Very Precious Love, The Loveliest Night of the Year, Raintree County, Memphis in June, Friendly Persuasion, April Love* and *Somewhere My Love*. Several of those numbers turned out to be more famous than the films for which they were written. One thinks of Paul only as a lyricist. In fact he collaborated in writing the music as well as the lyrics for many songs, including several of the above.

A number of his songs topped the Hit Parade, including *I Got It Bad (And That Ain't Good), Jump for Joy, Baltimore Oriole, The Twelfth of Never, A Certain Smile* and *The Green Leaves of Summer*.

Strange to say, in his middle years and thereafter for the rest of his life, this man, who in his younger days had led such a wild, adventurous life, became a confirmed homebody, almost a recluse. He was perfectly content to remain at home in his spacious house with its private pool and tennis court. He had almost no social life, rarely going to parties, although he was invited and was welcome everywhere. He left partying and social affairs to his scintillating wife, who reveled in them, and to his sons Guy and Roger.

An omnivorous reader and possessing an encyclopedic mind and memory, a true intellectual, he was to be found cloistered in his study day after day, absorbed in his books and music. With rare exceptions, his only visitors were the songwriters with whom he collaborated.

Closeted with them in his study, they worked often until three or four in the morning.

One year his son Guy, an inveterate world traveler, prevailed upon his father to go with him to Italy. Paul stayed for one week and then couldn't wait to fly home. His son was an avid skier and coaxed him to try skiing. But one day was more than enough for his father.

Awards and Hobbies

He was the winner of three Academy Awards or Oscars for the lyrics to *Secret Love* in 1953, *Love is a Many Splendored Thing* (co-author of both lyrics and music) in 1955; and *The Shadow of Your Smile* in 1965. During a career spanning over forty years, he wrote some 500 songs, received 16 Academy Award nominations, and earned 20 Gold Records and numerous other awards.

He was a member of the Academy of Motion Picture Arts and Sciences, of the Dramatist Guild, the Composers League of America, the Manuscript Society and other organizations. He was, as well, an officer of the American Society of Composers, Authors and Publishers (ASCAP).

He started his hobby of book-collecting at the age of sixteen. His rare and priceless collection of manuscripts and literary memorabilia included an original copy of the Magna Carta from 1299, a 1565 edition of *The Canterbury Tales*, first folios of Shakespeare plays, a copy of *The Pickwick Papers* of Dickens personally inscribed by Charles Dickens to Hans Christian Andersen, and a copy of Thackery's *Vanity Fair*, with Thackery's handwritten inscription to Charlotte Bronte.

A Serendipitous Discovery

The writer of this memoir had a pleasantly surprising experience related to one of Paul Webster's most celebrated songs. I happen to be a ham jazz pianist of sorts. Most of the tunes I play are the so-called popular "standards" of the 1930s, 1940s, 1950s, 1960s, etc., including tunes of Gershwin, Rogers & Hart, Rogers and Hammerstein, Cole Porter, Irving Berlin, Duke Ellington, Vincent Youmans, Arthur Schwartz, Bert Bachrach, and others. Like everyone else in my family, I was always aware that we had a famous cousin who had written many popular hits and theme songs for well-known motion pictures. But it never occurred to me that he wrote lyrics for "the master" himself–Duke Ellington. One day, while playing Ellington's *I Got It Bad (And That Ain't Good)*, I felt that my chord changes needed to be improved upon and decided to examine the actual score. I went to that unique institution–the New York Public Library Branch for the Performing Arts at Lincoln Center, which has the scores for virtually every piece of popular music ever written, got out the sheet music for *I Got It Bad*, and was astounded to see at the top of the page: "Music by Duke Ellington, Words by Paul Francis Webster."

And what marvelous words they are!!:

"Never treats me sweet and gentle
The way he should
I got it bad, and that ain't good!
My poor heart is sentimental
Not made of wood.
I got it bad, and that ain't good!
But when the weekend's over
And Monday rolls aroun'
I end up like I start out,
Just cryin' my heart out.
He don't love me like I love him
Nobody could
I got it bad, and that ain't good!"

Who but Paul Webster could have written those lyrics, at once so moving, so poignant, yet so simple and colloquial? He died at the age of seventy-five. His son Guy remarked of him, "He rarely left his beautiful home and his wonderful family except to attend meetings of ASCAP, to find a good salami sandwich, or to pick up an Academy Award."

CHAPTER VII

THE LIEBOWITZES

Early Immigrants

Fanny Unterberg, my mother's mother and my grandmother, came to America from Eastern Europe around 1875 as a girl of ten, together with her parents and a younger brother and sister. Her father got work as a mason, and the family lived in two crowded rooms on New York's lower East Side. A year later when her mother became ill with consumption, Fanny was obliged to quit school to shop, clean, cook and keep house for the family. She tried to educate herself by poring over her brother's school books at night. But she had to get up at six A.M. in a freezing house, start a fire, say her morning prayers and prepare breakfast for the family. A few years later her mother died.

At sixteen, now of marriageable age, she sat in the kitchen at night, sewing and darning, and listened to the talk of her father and the young men he brought to the house as suitors. The one that pleased her most was one who seemed learned, embellishing his conversation with sayings from the Talmud. He wasn't bad looking either, with blue eyes and a pleasant face. His name was Simon Liebowitz.

Simon came from a poor family near Riga, then part of Russia. His mother had wanted him to become a rabbi but he had to give up his studies to help support the family, initially by taking care of the stables and horses of a neighboring farmer, and later peddling pots, pans, ribbons and cloth around the countryside. While still a youth, when he was threatened with being conscripted into the czar's army, and after his parents had borrowed the money for steerage passage, he stole his way across the border to Germany and came to America. Now seven years later, as he looked at Fanny he said to himself, "At twenty-three, after all, a man should have a wife and his own home." A few months later they were married.

A Hard Working Family

They lived in three rooms. In one room they cooked and ate; in the second they slept, and in the third they cut and sewed piece goods into shirts, dresses and other garments. Their first child they named Abe, their second Harry. When Harry was eight days old Fanny was back at the sewing machine. They worked hard, saved and denied themselves everything to support their little business, which prospered and grew as the years passed.

There were now seven children, six boys and a girl. They had purchased a four-story house on East Broadway with the family occupying the basement and first floor. The three upper floors were leased out to tenants. The downstairs basement contained the dining room where the children did their lessons, a bathroom, a toilet and the kitchen with its iron stove and washtubs, and behind that a bedroom where the two oldest boys slept. Finally, in the rear there was a small cubbyhole where Emma, the Polish girl, slept. Upstairs there was a long narrow parlor with golden-haired cherubim painted on the high vaulted ceiling, and behind it the parents' bedroom. In the back there were two rooms for the four other boys and a tiny room for the daughter.

It was a busy household. At six-thirty in the morning Simon and the boys raced through their prayers. At seven A.M. Abe, the oldest son, having finished high school, accompanied his father to the shop. After that Fanny washed, dressed and gave the younger children their breakfast and the older boys were off to school. At eight A.M. the Hebrew teacher arrived to teach their daughter Sophie Hebrew, and shortly thereafter Fanny, already dressed, left for work on the horse car, but not before hurriedly giving Emma instructions about the day's cooking and other chores. Fanny often emphasized her instructions with one of the trite sayings of which she was very fond. "Don't think," she would tell Emma, "that just because we have a cellar full of coal that we are millionaires. Waste not want not, I always say!"

When she was gone, Sophie was left home to take care of her three younger brothers.

At night Simon was tired and sat in his chair reading his Yiddish newspaper. Fanny, a woman of enormous energy, her work never done, would be busy with the younger children, supervising the cooking, mending clothes and darning socks. Frequently a penniless new immigrant, fresh off the boat, sat in the kitchen asking Simon for advice as to what he should do to make a living, what merchandise he should try to peddle and where. If he had no other means, Simon might offer him a menial, low-paying job at the shop. If he complained, Fanny would favor him with another one of her

218

aphorisms: "You've got to start somewhere," she would say. Or "Where there's a will, there's a way." If he left in a huff, she would say to her husband: "You can't teach an old dog new tricks!"

There was no money as yet for summer holidays to the Jersey shore or the Catskills. Frequently on very hot summer evenings the whole family would go down to the foot of Grand Street and ride the ferry on the East River all night to keep cool.

Striving for Culture and Amusement

Although she had little schooling, Fanny had a great respect for education and culture. She persisted and taught herself to read and write, and later in life became an avid reader. Abe was obliged to take piano lessons, and Harry and Ephie (Ephraim) violin lessons. At night and on weekends the house reverberated with a cacophony of pounding on the piano and the squeaking of the violin. None of the children exhibited any sign of musical genius and eventually the lessons were discontinued. Still, at his Bar Mitzvah party when he was thirteen, Harry bravely struggled through a short Schumann piece with his teacher accompanying him on the piano, while Fanny beamed with pride. Later on, Sophie was given dancing and elocution lessons.

Busy as she was, Fanny was never too tired to go out and have a good time when the opportunity arose, although it was always difficult to persuade Simon to accompany her. The big social event of the season was the Annual Ball of the Ladies Fuel and Aid Society, held

Fanny Liebowitz

uptown at Madison Square Garden. "Mama's gown," her daughter Sophie recalled, "had a train that swept the floor. Busts were large, hips were generous and bodices heavily boned and smartly drawn in at the waistline to give it that fulsome rounded look so admired by the ladies." After being helped by the maid to step into two petticoats and carefully pulling her dress over her head, all the little invisible hooks and eyes that went down the back to below the waist were hooked up. "Now in her long, black velvet dress, her white shoulders gleaming, a necklace of shiny stones at her throat, her black, wavy hair piled high on her head, Mama looked handsome and young."

The greatest form of pleasure for Fanny was going to the Yiddish theater to see the great tragedies of Yiddish drama or of Shakespeare performed by Jacob Adler, Madame Bertha Kalish or other luminaries, or to cry or laugh at the sentimental melodramas and comedies so dear to Jewish audiences. Simon invariably was too tired to go, so that it was usually her daughter Sophie, to her great delight, who accompanied her mother on these occasions.

A Growing Business, New Problems

Initially Simon and Fanny's brother Israel Unterberg were partners. Later "Uncle Izzy" left to start his own shirt business. Now with his three older sons at work with him and the business growing rapidly, Simon changed the name to "S. Liebowitz and Sons, Inc." Then came several crises that threatened to put them out of business altogether. First came a strike by their employees –cutters, steam ironers, swatch-makers and the girls in the sewing department–for higher wages. Simon and his sons insisted that if wages were raised they would go out of business. Fanny felt that they would have to grant an increase, but she also had a solution. "If the men's shirts, which had long skirts almost like nightgowns, were cut differently, with shorter skirts and fitting closer to the body, a half-dozen inches of material would be saved with each shirt." Simon wisely followed his wife's advice, increased his workers' wages and the strike ended; and as Fanny had predicted, the change in shirt patterns resulted in a lower cost of piece goods that more than made up for the increased labor costs.

Then came the panic of 1893 and two years of depression that followed. Like most other concerns, the Liebowitz business relied on loans from banks and credit from suppliers, with repayment occurring normally as the finished garments were shipped and paid for. Now the banks refused credit and the cotton mills declined to ship piece goods. The family suddenly saw their life's work threatened with the prospect of bankruptcy. Again Fanny came to the rescue. She took the initiative and went alone to see the owner of the mill that was their major supplier, told him at great length how hard they had worked, supplied him with figures of their growing sales volume, their production costs, margin of profit, and their long record of honesty and integrity. He was persuaded to renew their line of credit and the problem was solved.

Summer Vacations

For years the Liebowitz family, like everyone else living on the lower East Side, spent their summer months in the sweltering city, sitting on their stoops or on chairs on the sidewalks at night, grateful for an occasional breeze from the river. One day her sister-in-law, Belle Unterberg, said to Fanny, "You ought to take your children to the country. Look at your daughter Sophie! She's as thin as a broomstick!" Fanny agreed. The family finances had now improved and Fanny, resolved that the children must have the benefit of fresh air, fresh milk and fresh vegetables, announced that they would spend next summer on a farm. "But what will we do there?" the boys exclaimed. "Never mind," Fanny said, "a healthy body, a healthy mind, I always say!"

Fanny scrutinized the classified ads in the newspapers the next spring and found a place called "Haines Farm" in northern New Jersey, complete with cows, horses, chickens, ducks and pigs, a big barn and hayloft, and an old-fashioned well from which a bucket brought up ice-cold water. Aunt Mary, Simon's spinster sister, was persuaded to stay there with the children. Mama and Papa, busy all week in the business, took turns coming there on weekends, bringing kosher meat.

The following summer Fanny decided that the place for the children was the Jersey shore at Long Branch and found a boarding house, the "Ocean View Hotel" recommended by one of her friends, that even served kosher meals. "And such food!" Fanny was told, "It just melts in your mouth!" Fanny and Simon would come down from the city on Friday night for the weekend.

During the week, Sophie was responsible for looking after her three younger brothers.

The boys had one-piece, striped, bathing-suits. Sophie's was of blue wool that covered her from the neck to below the knees, with a shirt that reached her ankles. Fanny bought everything several sizes too large so that it would be good for future summers. When Sophie complained, her mother said, "The way you're growing, by next summer it will be too small for you!"

"Mama's bathing-suit of heavy poplin," Sophie recalled, "had been made by a dressmaker and fitted her well. Underneath, her natural curves were decorously held in by a heavily boned corset. The suit covered her bosom and arms, long black stockings encased her feet, and a Mother-Hubbard bathing hat covered her hair. Papa remained on the front porch of the hotel. He loathed sea-water bathing, and could never understand why people were willing to dress and undress several times a day to swim in the ocean."

Years later, when the shirt business had made the Liebowitzes well-to-do, Simon and Uncle Izzy Unterberg purchased large adjoining mansions in Arverne, Long Island, a half block from the ocean. It was here, on the Arverne beach, that one day Sophie was introduced to Cecil Ruskay, her future husband.

75 Leonard Street

As the business continued to prosper, Simon moved the family to larger and more sumptuous quarters uptown, first to a house on East 70th Street and later on to a large brownstone on West 89th Street, just off Central Park West.

Meanwhile, the family enterprise that had started years before as a tiny home operation and then progressed to a small shop, was now located downtown in a large four-story loft building which Simon had bought at 75 Leonard Street. On the first floor were desks for the salesmen, clerks and stenographers and private offices for the bosses. A huge elevator operated by steel cables carried freight and personnel to the upper floors. On the third floor Fanny presided over girls sitting at sewing machines making ladies' garments and nightgowns with long sleeves, drawers and petticoats with deep ruffles. Skilled "cutters" cut rolls of piece goods at long tables on one part of the fourth floor, while elsewhere, pressers ironed men's dress shirts and long nightgowns (pajamas were not yet in vogue). Shipping and mailing operations were conducted on the second floor.

Abe strolled about the ground floor examining the orders and supervising the clerical help, a big cigar in his mouth, talking to Arthur Rothstein, the firm's star salesman, who was paid $25,000 a year, an unheard of amount in those days. Ephie was the office manager, who bought supplies and supervised the bookkeepers. He prided himself on his economies. An office joke had it that Ephie retrieved, saved and reused paper clips, rubber bands and wrapping paper.

Meanwhile Harry, who made the big decisions, sat in an aerie above the top floor, where he oversaw production at the firm's Pennsylvania factories in Meyerstown, Pottstown and Kutztown, which were now all unionized. When problems arose with the workers in the factories, Harry would go out to the plants to handle them. He was a good speaker, forceful and sincere. Harry wasn't handsome but he wasn't unattractive either. Still, with his plainly semitic features, he must have appeared to these common folk as the epitome, perhaps even the caricature, of the Jewish boss from New York. But when he climbed up on a cutting table and calmly addressed several hundred workers on a factory floor, he invariably gained their attention and respect.

Men's dress shirts and nightwear continued to pour out of the Liebowitz factories. S. Liebowitz & Sons, Inc. was now big business. By the late 1930s it was the largest manufacturer, in terms of volume though not in dollar amount of sales, in the country, eclipsing even the giant Arrow and Van Heusen companies.

Relatives, Poor and Otherwise

Simon, in addition to his two sisters, had two brothers and a number of uncles and aunts, all poor an unemployed, many of them recent arrivals from Europe who spoke little English. Fanny regarded them all as "loafers" but Simon felt responsible for them. For those would could work, he found menial jobs in the business at Leonard Street; and for the others he arranged secretly to send them every month small stipends to pay their rent or other necessities, with his daughter Sophie, now seventeen, usually serving as his emissary on these missions. Actually Fanny knew quite well what was going on but said nothing.

Simon also had problems with his sisters. Initially, with the help of a matchmaker, he had to find husbands for them. Later, when the marriage failed, he was obliged to go to the trouble and expense of persuading a rabbi to give them a "get," a ritual Jewish divorce. Finally, one day Fanny lost patience and burst out: "Show me another man who has as many sisters, brothers, uncles and aunts who are all such schlemiels! I know that one should honor one's father and mother and provide for them in their old age. But where, I ask, is it written that you must look after brothers and sisters and other relatives who hang on to you like leeches and can do nothing for themselves?"

"If they were otherwise," Simon replied, "would they need me? Besides, the Talmud says, 'Hide not thyself from they kinsfolk.'"

Fanny did not answer. Who was she to question the Talmud and other rabbinical authorities?

Another relative, Grandpa Unterberg, Fanny's father, used to come to the house to visit occasionally, but always alone. He was a tall man, vigorous for his age, gentle and kind and proud of the fact that he still worked as a mason and builder. He used to take his granddaughter Sophie for walks and treat her to ice-cream, roast chestnuts and other goodies. One day he took her to visit his little flat on Allen Street, where the door was opened by a plump little woman in a long black dress with an elaborately embroidered apron, who had on her head a sheitl, the ritual wig worn by pious Jewish women. Sophie then realized that this was her grandfather's second wife, whom he had married when Fanny's mother died. Fanny, who had worshiped her mother, never forgave him and never allowed him to set foot in her house.

The Older Brothers' Families

Abe, Harry and Ephie all married handsome women from good middle-class Jewish families. Their wives didn't always seem to get along very well with one another. Etta, Harry's wife, several times threatened to leave him for reasons no one could discover. But Fanny, the quintessential mother hen, always intervened and managed to patch things up. Etta was also parsimonious. The rest of the family was always amused by the fact that although Harry gave her a generous allowance for household expenses, on Sundays she would announce that there was no food in the house and send Harry trudging around the corner to the delicatessen for sandwiches. We always suspected that Etta would squirrel away the money saved for other purposes.

Ephie was quite handsome as a young man, and his wife Reda was unusually lovely. Tall, slender, with an aquiline nose and a long slender neck that reminded one of a swan, she was as gracious and charming as she was beautiful. She was a particular favorite of my mother Sophie. Tragically, while still in her thirties, she came down with streptococcus throat and died after a brief illness. Penicillin, which was discovered a year or two later, would have saved her life.

The older brothers were exemplary sons and affectionate uncles. Harry was particularly generous. Later in life he gave $5,000 worth of preferred stock in

S. Liebowitz & Sons, Inc. to each of the children of his sister Sophie and of his younger brothers.

The Younger Brothers

Unlike their older brothers who went to work in the family business right after graduation from high school, the three younger Liebowitz sons were sent to college with the expectation that they would make careers for themselves in one of the professions or as teachers.

Sidney graduated from Columbia with a Ph.D in chemistry and for some time taught chemistry in high school. He also became involved in a number of business projects designed to exploit his ideas for new chemical products, with his parents supplying the financing, each of them a disastrous failure. A mild, quiet man and a bachelor for years, Fanny eventually found him a wife, and his parents set up a trust fund for his benefit in return for his promise to forego any further ventures into the world of business. It was not a happy marriage. His wife, Florence, was always unsatisfied, jealous of her wealthier sisters-in-law, and eventually they were divorced.

Ben received his Ph.D in Physics, also from Columbia. For a while he worked for Thomas Edison in New Jersey. Later he was employed by the family shirt business to do a survey of their Pennsylvania factories to increase the efficiency of their operations, and was responsible for the installation of new sprinkler systems and a number of labor-saving improvements. But for most of his life he was an independent physicist. He had a fine scientific mind and became a friend of Leo Szillard, Robert Oppenheimer and other members of the group at Columbia that worked on the Manhattan Project for the manufacture of the A-bomb.

For years he lived in an apartment uptown in Washington Heights with his wife Virginia and his children. Virginia, strange to say, was as plain looking as Ben was handsome, but she was brainy, well-educated and had a hearty sense of humor that matched her husband's. I lived with them for several months one winter while attending law school, and was treated like a member of the family. In contrast to the households of some of the other brothers, the atmosphere in the Ben Liebowitz home was always lively and gay.

Years later Ben discovered and patented a method of fusing the collar materials attached to men's shirts so that they remained semi-stiff without starching, even after being washed. The new method, which he called "Trubenizing," was widely adopted by the industry and made him a millionaire. But he never changed his unpretentious lifestyle.

Shortly after World War I, David, the youngest of the Liebowitz sons, then an ensign in the navy, over six feet tall and looking very handsome in his officer's uniform, was married in the parlor of his parents' West 89th Street home to Emily Gresser. Emily, a gifted young violinist, a friend of Jascha Heifitz, Mischa Elman and other celebrated musicians, who had already made a name for herself as a concert artist, gave up what promised to be a brilliant career for marriage and family life. If she ever regretted it, this gentle, charming woman never let on, unselfishly devoting herself to her husband

and children. Although she occasionally played chamber music in her home before an audience of friends, accompanied by her brothers and other accomplished musicians, she never set foot on a concert stage again.

David was an intellectual, an art connoisseur and a writer. He numbered among his distinguished friends Franz Boaz the anthropologist, Lewis Mumford the authority on architecture and city planning, the painter John Marin and other prominent persons in the intellectual and artistic world. Although he wrote several novels, short stories and plays, he was eventually frustrated as a writer. However he lived to see his daughter, Bettina L. Knapp, Professor of Romance Languages and Comparative Literature at Hunter College, a prolific writer strongly influenced by her father, publish a series of brilliant biographies and psychological studies, including those of actors and writers in the French theatrical and literary world, twenty-six at last count, not to mention numerous articles in scholarly journals and magazines.

David was a colorful, interesting personality, not at all bashful about expressing his aesthetic views in public. One night my parents gave me their tickets to the Metropolitan Opera and asked me to invite my uncle David. The opera was Wagner's "Das Rheingold," and our seats were in the front row of the first balcony. David sat back and made himself comfortable by stretching out his long legs and resting them on the guard rail. When the people in back of us complained that he was obstructing their view of the stage, he turned around and said, "Surely you don't want to watch these obese and ungainly Rhine maidens cavort about the

Stage! Why don't you just close your eyes and listen to the music?"

The Unterbergs

Fanny was very close to her older brother, Israel Unterberg. Uncle Izzy, as he was called by the Liebowitz children, at one time a partner with Simon, had long since established a successful shirt and pajama business of his own. In addition, he had had the foresight to invest in downtown Manhattan real estate and became very rich. He was tall and impressive looking, with a drooping white mustached, very dignified, even a little pompous, and very proud of the fact that, by virtue of his membership on the boards of the Young Men's Hebrew Association and various other Jewish charitable organizations, he rubbed shoulders with sundry Warburgs, Lehmans and Schiffs and other members of the old German-Jewish investment banking families.

Uncle Izzy had moved his family uptown, out of the crowded tenement area of the lower East Side, long before the Liebowitzes had left East Broadway for more spacious and genteel quarters on East 70th Street. As a result, for years the atmosphere in the Unterberg home was as quiet and sedate as the Liebowitz's was noisy and hectic. Aunt Belle, Uncle Izzy's wife, presided over her brood of two sons and five daughters like a queen, and was waited on hand-and-foot by her adoring family.

Their cousin Sophie was always very popular with the Unterberg girls and frequently slept over in their home.

Israel Unterberg

At meals, Sophie recalled, Uncle Izzy sat at the head of the table with Aunt Belle next to him. "Uncle always addressed his wife as 'My love,' and his hand, when not engaged in eating or cutting up the food for the younger children, would be lovingly patting hers. Everyone was well behaved and the service was quiet and orderly. Yet I missed the noisy arguments at our own table at home. Uncle would carefully wipe the silky fringe of his drooping mustache after every course, a performance that never ceased to fascinate me. Then before dessert was served, he would clear his throat.

"'My love,'" he would begin as he again patted Aunt Belle's little hand, 'I am afraid that according to their report cards, some of the girls have been very negligent in their studies this last week!' As the guilty parties made as if they were about to burst into tears, Aunt Belle would come to the rescue and say, 'I'm sure they do better than most others!'

"Then Uncle would give up, pat his wife's hand again and say, 'Alright, my love, it can wait. I will go over their homework with them tonight.' Then Aunt Belle would change the subject and inquire: 'How was the conference at the hospital this morning?' and Uncle, brightening visibly, would describe with great pride his meeting that day with his distinguished associates."

Sophie also remembered how, late at night when the household was asleep, she was startled to see the tall figure of her uncle, barefoot and clad only in a long night shirt, going quietly from room to room, adjusting the covers of the children before quietly leaving.

The Unterbergs were perceived to be, and perhaps considered themselves, somewhat more genteel than their Liebowitz cousins, The family shirt and pajama business, for example, was never considered suitable for Clarence, the favorite son, tall like his father and exceedingly handsome. Instead he was sent down to Wall Street where he established a large brokerage and securities firm.

It was common knowledge that a sort of pecking order existed among New York's upper- and middle-class Jewish families that was somewhat analogous to what existed in Boston society, where the Cabots and Lodges were reputed to speak only to one another. Here in the city, the families of Russian and other East European Jews, like the Unterbergs and Liebowitzes, occupied the lowest rung on the social ladder, and above them were those whose forebears had come from Germany, like the Loebs, Lehmans, Schiffs, Warburgs and other investment banking families. At the top were the Cardozos, the Solis-Cohens, the Nathans and other Spanish-Portuguese or Sephardic Jews whose origins had been in Spain and who were the earliest members of the Chosen People to settle in America.

And so it was that when Edgar J. Nathan Jr., whose father had been a law partner of Benjamin Cardozo before he became a Supreme Court Judge, met and married the dark-eyed beauty Mabel Unterberg, Uncle Izzy's daughter, the way was clear for the entire Unterberg family, or at least all of those who attended synagogues and who, like the Liebowitzes, had worshiped for years at the Society for the Advancement of Judaism on West 86th Street presided over by the eminent Rabbi Mordecai Kaplan, now to transfer their allegiance to the Spanish-Portuguese Synagogue on

Central Park West, where the pulpit was occupied by the equally prominent Rabbi David de Sola Pool.

The Liebowitz Brothers Make a Mistake

In 1941, before the United States entered World War II, S. Liebowitz & Sons had reached the peak of its success, with hundreds of important department stores and retail establishments all over the United States as faithful customers. In addition, it supplied an important part of the shirt and pajama requirements of the two big mail order houses, Sears Roebuck and Montgomery Ward, affixing the Sears and the Montgomery Ward labels to the merchandise made specially for them. This production for Sears and Montgomery Ward represented a major segment of the Liebowitz output and was essential to keep their factories at full production.

When the United States entered the war the shirt industry, like so many others, faced a severe crisis. Piece goods for shirts and pajamas was hard to obtain because so much was needed to supply clothing for the armed forces. The Liebowitz retailers, chain store and department store customers clamored for merchandise. But so did Sears and Montgomery Ward, who made it clear that if the Liebowitz firm would fill their requirements, they would show their gratitude by continuing their large volume purchases after the war. Forced to choose, the brothers made a fatal error and funneled a major portion of their now diminished production to the two mail order houses. The result was that they not only lost the good will of hundreds of faithful retailers all over the country, but what was perhaps more important, used their reduced production to, in effect, advertise the Sears and Montgomery Ward names instead of using it to promote the S. Liebowitz name and trademarks on merchandise which would have otherwise been displayed on retailer and department store counters. To make matters worse, the two giant mail order houses, far from showing their gratitude after the war when merchandise was again plentiful, pressured the Liebowitzes into granting them price and other concessions which made doing business with them only marginally profitable, and often not profitable at all. It was a mistake from which the firm never fully recovered.

Fanny, The Last Years

Throughout her life Fanny was the cement, the lynchpin, that held her family together. It was she who acted as arbiter of the occasional disputes in the business between the brothers; she who somehow managed to smooth over the petty differences that arose between their wives. Simon, her husband, had passed away; the big house on West 89th Street had been sold; and she now lived alone with a maid in an apartment on Central Park West. Now in her seventies she no longer, as she had done for so many years, rode downtown with her chauffeur Kennedy to see for herself what was going on at 75 Leonard Street. Now her time was devoted largely to visiting her various grandchildren in the city, Westchester and Long Island to inquire about their schooling and other activities.

She nevertheless remained active in a number of charitable organizations, including the Ladies Fuel and Aid Society, of which she was now the president. Sophie remembered dropping in for a visit one day and seeing her mother through a half-opened door, standing in another room rehearsing the address that she was to deliver the next day at a meeting of the Society. With Fanny was one of her older granddaughters, my sister Blix, already in college, who was going over the speech with her, line by line, explaining what words to emphasize, where to pause, even the hand gestures she might employ.

Moreover, she still prepared in her kitchen from time to time with the help of her maid, her special brand of gefilte fish and its jellied gravy, which she would have her chauffeur Kennedy deliver to her sons' homes. Gefilte fish mavens who sampled it insisted that there was none better anywhere. However I learned that the pleasure of eating this traditional Jewish delicacy when it is served at the dinner table is one thing; and that being in the vicinity during its preparation from ingredients of carp, pike, whitefish (the fish heads, bone and skin were cooked with the fish and separated out later), onions, carrots, parsley, clove garlic, eggs, salt and pepper, is something else. One night I happened to sleep over in my grandmother's apartment, occupying the sofa in the living room. The next morning Fanny and the maid were cooking gefilte fish in the kitchen. I awoke to be greeted by a smell that was so overpoweringly pungent, noisome and malodorous that I scrambled hastily into my clothes and dashed out the door into the fresh air, without even saying goodbye.

At the end of each day, her son Harry, "My Harry," as she called him, her unquestioned favorite, would drop by for a visit and tell her what had happened downtown at the business that day. He never failed her.

At seventy-five Fanny became seriously ill. The once large, powerful body seemed to have shriveled, her eyes were deeply sunken and her speech was scarcely audible. She now had, in addition to Kennedy and the maid, a Mrs. Weston, a kind and very competent woman as a full-time nurse. It was a pitiful sight to see Kennedy carrying the now fragile body from the bed to her armchair. Sophie would come every day and her sons would drop in in the evening. She lingered for a few weeks and then died peacefully in her sleep at the age of seventy-six.

Now it was Sophie, a very energetic and busy woman herself, who replaced her mother as a sort of family watchdog. She had played this role for years with regard to her brothers and their wives. Now it was their children and grandchildren and their occasional problems that engaged her interest.

One by one her brothers died. Sophie, who lived to be ninety-six, survived them all. But in the end neither Fanny nor her daughter ever succeeded in bringing the disparate threads of the Liebowitz family together. Just as the wives of the various brothers had never betrayed much interest in their sisters-in-law, the same was largely true of their children and grandchildren.

The interests of the Liebowitzes and their older sons were focused almost entirely, first on establishing and later on expanding, the family business. Although they gave generously to their synagogue and to Jewish philanthropies, unlike my father's family, the Baums, Websters, Crohns, Epsteins et al., they never entered into the public life of the city, or played leading roles in the bustling world of community and Jewish affairs.

And unlike my father's relatives, there were no periodic large family parties or reunions, no sense of family, no geniality or gaiety. When Sophie died, the last link between the members of the succeeding generation disappeared. To this day Fanny and Simon's grandchildren and great-grandchildren rarely, if ever, see one another, unaware of and uninterested in one another's existence.

The End of the Business

After World War II, S. Liebowitz and Sons, Inc., now more intent on broadening its market for its Truval and Essley brand of shirts, changed its name to what the brothers considered the more distinguished name of Publix Shirt Corporation and moved uptown to a more fashionable address in the Empire State Building.

Either because there was some falling out between the brothers or because, unlike Harry or Ephie, he had neither a son nor son-in-law ready to take his place, Abe, now well along in years, arranged to have his brothers buy out his interest in the business and retired. As time passed Harry and Ephie, as well, passed away, and Robert, Ephie's son, and Sheldon Burden, Harry's son-in-law, both very competent, took over the management. By now the nature of the business had changed. It had become more competitive than ever.

Dress shirts, which were the chief product before the war, now occupied a distant second place to sports shirts, as informality in the workplace became more and more the vogue.

The firm continued to prosper but it never regained the dominant position that it had occupied in the industry during the pre-war period. Eventually Robert and Sheldon, by now veterans themselves, began to think of retirement from the fray, and when the opportunity arrived they arranged for the business to be sold, and the great name of S. Liebowitz & Sons, Inc., became only a distant memory.

AFTERWORD

I have always been aware that my forebears, especially those on my fathers side of the family, going back to the middle of the nineteenth century–and even earlier–were an interesting, colorful and congenial lot and included some truly unusual people, such as Abbe Baum, Dr. Burrill Crohn, Esther J. Ruskay and Judith Epstein. Their accomplishments, along with those of other early members of the so-called Baum-Webster clan and its Crohn, Ruskay, Epstein and other offshoots, were periodically recalled and celebrated at large family parties with speeches, songs, stories and poetry, both serious and light-hearted. Moreover, some years ago an excellent compendium, *The Saga of the Baum-Webster Family Tree*, containing in considerable detail virtually all that was known of the family's history, was compiled by two of Abbe Baum's grandchildren, and provided the descendants of Abbe and Jacob ("Yank") Webster with a wealth of information about their antecedents, starting with the first to arrive here from Eastern Europe in 1842.

Still, until recently, Abbe and other family icons were for me little more than dim figures of the distant past, venerated by the family, but about whom I had only the vaguest knowledge. Then one day my cousin Ruth Dickler, Burrill Crohn's daughter, allowed me to browse through her collection of family pictures, letters and other memorabilia, some of them over one hundred and fifty years old. Suddenly I came across a photograph, a copy of which had hung for years in my parents' home and which I had entirely forgotten. It was a picture of my father's mother, Esther J. Ruskay, a writer, essayist and prominent public figure. She was shown seated at a small table situated, of all places, at the front opening of a large platform tent on the ocean beach at Arverne, Long Island, where her family, then in straitened circumstances, was spending the summer months. Fully dressed and as composed as if she had been in her New York City living room, she was busily engaged in attending to her voluminous correspondence with leading men and women in the world of Jewish affairs. Then I came upon the lengthy *New York Times* obituary of my cousin, the late Judith Epstein, the revered elder stateswoman of Hadassah, and my mind traveled back in time some sixty-five years to the year 1923. It was then, as a boy of thirteen, that I had heard Judith, then an attractive young matron, speak for the first time, electrifying an audience in Far Rockaway, Long Island, with her brilliant oratory. Finally, and perhaps most impressive, were the writings of Ruth's father the late Dr. Burrill Crohn, the discoverer of Crohn's Disease, who had achieved world-wide notoriety when President Eisenhower was afflicted with that malady. These included *Notes on the Evolution of a Medical Specialist*, as well as some of his colorful memoranda about the huge Crohn family and his early Baum-Webster relatives.

It was then at my cousin's home, during that pleasant nostalgia trip through the past, that the thought occurred to me of writing a memoir about aspects of this family's history. It would surely be of interest to hundreds of my relatives and more recent members of the family tree–the physicians, lawyers, members of academia, musicians and business people, and their families. But beyond that, it seemed to me that the activities and accomplishments of some of these early family members, many of them deeply involved in the public life of the city, should be of interest to a wider audience than that of their own relatives and descendants. Moreover, the story of their lives in a much smaller, simpler and more provincial nineteenth century New York, seemed representative of the struggle of the early immigrants from Europe, strangers in a new land, to lift themselves into the more comfortable middle class, and to pursue lives of intelligent and enlightened citizenship.

As for the very young, the children of the '80s and '90s, including my teen-age grandchildren, whether the character and lives of their distinguished antecedents will make a significant impression upon them, I wonder. Perhaps their involvement in the world of computers, software and fax machines, not to mention MTV and the current taste in what passes these days for literature, will cause them to look upon the lives of these figures of the past as only mildly interesting and quaint, at best. However, one can always hope.

JOSEPH UNTERBERG ('ZADIG) M. ZEPOISAH

ISRAEL UNTERBERG M. BELLE EPSTEIN

FAMILY UNTERBERG M. SIMON LIEBOWITZ

SYLVIA M. M. EIKIND

MABEL M. EDWARD NATHAN JR.

D... M. M. A. WELL

DAVID M.

LILLIAN M. SIM ROSENTHAL

GERTRUDE "GERT" M. UNTERBERG

ADELE

ABRAHAM M. HANNAH

HARRY M. ETTA

EPHRAIM "EPHIE" M. DEBORAH

SADIE M. LEECH MORAY

BENJAMIN M. VIRGINIA

SIDNEY M. FRIEDAE

DAVID M. EMILY

BEATRICE M. LAWRENCE AND DIMICEL HOLMAN

SYLVIA M. E. BENNETT

RUTH M. WILLIAM ROSENMAN

JOY M. SHERMAN JACTON

RACHEL M. JANET

HARVEY M. SAMUEL JOSEPH

DAVID M. MYRA SIMON

ESTHER "ALEX" M. H. ARNOLD

JOSEPH M. MARCY SITNER

JULIE ALEX AND ROGER SITNER

EVERETT M. JEAN & FRANKEL

CECELIA M. A. KAHZ

NAOMI M.

ELSBETH

JONATHAN

DANIEL M.

BETTINA M. ROBERT LAHOFF

BAUM-WEBSTER FAMILY TREE (LO PAH AS PENTIMENT)

ISRAEL BAUM M. LENA OLSON (1851-1895) (1860-1946)

JESSE "JAY" VON WEBBER, SENNENHBUREN (1870-1886 1965) (1867-1933)

- REBECCA
- GERTRUDE
- MILLIE
- DAISY
- ESTER
- DORA
- ANTHONY

- RAY
- DAVID
- JEROME
- SIDNEY
- JANE m. JAKE JOANNE
- MYRON m. BLANCHE JEANNE
- JANE
- ETHEL HARRY
- LESLIE

MARTON — PAUL M.
- GUY
- ROGER

ABE BAUM M. GOLDIE WEBSTER (1878-1901)

- JOSHUA (SCHMULY)
- ESTHER m. SAMUEL RUSKIN
- LEAH (1877-1933) m. THEODORE CRONER
- REBECCA
- MILLICENT 1883-1943
- SARA m. EDDIE MARTIN
- ISAAC
- JACOB
- MINNIE
- DAVID m. ETTA

- RUTH
- BREVIL
- EVERETT
- CECIL m. SOPHIE LIEBOWITZ
  - ESTHER (CELIA) m. HARVEY BRESSLER
  - LESTER m. MARGOT STEIN
  - ELIZABETH m. WILHELM and LOUISE PURCELL
  - EVERETT m. PEGGY LIPSCHUTZ
  - CECILE m. ARTHUR G. SCHATZ

- NAOMI m. MORRIS P. EPSTEIN
- JUDITH m. ELIZABETH née FOOTE
- ABE m. JEWISH SOMEONE and SOMEONE

- DAVID M. SYLVIA
- NAOMI m. L. COHEN
- DAVID M.
- EVELYN M.

- ESTHER m. DR. SHAPIRO
  - RUTH m. GERALD DISCHLER
  - EDWARD m. FRANCIS
- BURRILL m. and PEGG and ROSE EDELGLAST
- ADA MAY
- GERDA m. M. ROTH
- MYRON
- JOSHUA
- NAOMI
- LAWRENCE
- DANIEL
- JEROME
- ANN-CELIA m. A. RIEL
- JULIE